THE SUCCESSFUL MANAGER

Also by William R. Van Dersal

The Successful Supervisor in Government and Business

THE
SUCCESSFUL
MANAGER
in Government
and Business

by William R. Van Dersal

HARPER & ROW, PUBLISHERS

NEW YORK, EVANSTON
SAN FRANCISCO
LONDON

1817

FIRST EDITION

Designed by Lydia Link

Library of Congress Cataloging in Publication Data

Van Dersal, William Richard, 1907-
   The successful manager in government and business.
   Bibliography: p.
   Includes index.
   1. Management.   I. Title.
HD31.V318   1975   658.4   74-1864
ISBN 0-06-014488-2

Contents

Preface

THIS BOOK was conceived and written for managers in government, industry, business, education, and other fields. It offers ideas, techniques, and approaches that I believe have proven to be more successful in operation than many of the usual practices. It does not seek to tell managers what they should or should not do, or how they should operate, or that they should change from what they are now doing to something else. The principal objective of the book is to help managers think about or consider a number of ideas that may help them in managing their unit or organization.

I am quite sure that none of the ideas in this book is new. They are, rather, ways of approaching the management of operations that both managers and supervisors have used successfully in recent years and that correlate reasonably well with the newest and latest scientific discoveries in the field of human behavior, particularly in organizations. Some of the material has been published in books and professional journals. Some of it has been available only in multilithed or mimeographed form. And some of it has never appeared in print.

It is obvious that there are great differences among organizations with respect to functional assignments at different levels, delegation of authority, staffing, and the service or product produced. It follows that we may have managers in one company or agency with quite different responsibilities from those at comparable levels in other companies or agencies. Thus, generalizing about "managers" is probably neither possible nor terribly useful.

On the other hand, managers of all kinds, in all sorts of organizations, face certain common problems of operation. Most of these problems concern getting people to do what is wanted by the organization—and at the highest achievable efficiency. This idea has two aspects—one relating to human behavior in work situations, and the other relating to the efficiency of the systems used. Parenthetically, the word "systems" is used here in the perfectly ordinary sense of doing something in an orderly way, rather than in the much used special senses of "systems analysis" or of "systems" involving computer operation. When a system is described in this book it has to do with a regular, orderly plan or method of procedure or arrangement that will get jobs done with little or no wasted effort.

With these two ideas in mind—human behavior and systematic operation—we are, I think, on common ground for managers in general. Government, business, industry, and other types of organizations are all pretty much in the same boat here. As shown by many studies, human behavior is similar both in different organizations in the same country and in different countries.

Systematic operation makes for success anywhere. Many people have assumed that operations in "government" as opposed to "industry and business" are quite different from one another, and therefore must be approached differently. But for many functions, this assumption is not correct. Red tape and waste are to be found in any and every type of organization. Training, communications, career development, organizational climates, conferences, supervision, staff operation, reporting, and many other functions or systems of operation are all common to government agencies, companies, industrial concerns, educational and religious institutions, and almost any other organization. The subject matter will necessarily be different, but the orderly or systematic approach is certainly not.

There really ought not to be any great difficulty with these ideas. It is true you cannot compare an entire "government" in general with a "private industry" as so many people are fond of doing. But governments are not single entities. The executive branch of the United States federal government, for example, is a cluster of agencies: the Forest Service, Soil Conservation Service, Park Service, Geological Survey, Bureau of Public Roads, Bureau of Public Debt, Bonneville Power Administration, and many more, adding up to some 200 organizations plus a sizable number of nearly autonomous regional offices. Such clusters are also present in large industrial or business concerns or conglomerates in which various units, subsidiary companies, or branch offices are essentially autonomous, at least insofar as management is concerned.

So, we can compare a single government agency under one directing head with a single company that is under one directing head. I am well aware that agencies are responsive to secretarial, executive, or Congressional policy, just as companies are responsive to interlocking or associated boards of directors. Even so, given two organizations with distinct and discrete programs or operating objectives, each operating under the direction of a single executive, the management of such agencies or concerns can very well be compared. Even here, it is wise to consider size (in terms of numbers of employees) and degree of decentralization. Just as it is scarcely useful to compare a small family business with a giant corporation, so it is of little use to compare a small regulatory government agency with a giant conglomerate dealing in electric power or dam construction.

Incidentally, the objectives of most government agencies (federal, state, municipal, or local) have to do with providing services of one kind or another to the public or to specific segments of the public. Private business and industrial concerns have similar objectives, despite beliefs to the contrary. Many people think of an industry or business as engaged solely in making money. Government agencies, on the other hand, they will tell you, do not have a profit motive. And yet the fact is that most government agencies must show a reasonable return for the money expended, just as must any business. If they don't they get reorganized or eliminated. And businesses that fail to provide real services to the public have trouble staying in business. Similarly, a manufactured product requires servicing, and the better the product and the better the servicing, the better the company looks to the public and the greater its profits.

A distinguished editor of Oxford University Press—the oldest publishing company in the world—once told me that "Oxford is in the business of disseminating information to the English-speaking people of the world. And in doing this, they have made a good deal of money." Service first, but profit second, dependent on service.

Most of this book is what is often described as "low key." The application of highly sophisticated systems to human beings, in the present state of our knowledge, is of doubtful value. It is still quite possible for people in an organization to say that if a man can't or doesn't get the job done, we replace him with another. This kind of attitude leads in turn to statements like "We've had six production managers in the last 18 months" or "Turnover rates in our concern are high because we mean business!" If you apply this theory (classed long ago as the "replacement theory"[1]) to an automobile that can't or won't run, you'd end up getting a new one every time you ran out of gas. Managers, supervisors, and workers may not get the job done for a variety of reasons. Application of sophisticated systems does not seem to be as wise as

---

1. In *Group Dynamics—Key to Decision-Making*, by Robert R. Blake and Jane S. Mouton. Houston, Texas: Gulf Publishing Co., 1961.

finding out *why*, since organizational conditions, rather than the man, may be responsible. This means that the practical man who came up through the ranks without sophisticated training had better forget that he is uneducated, and the college man had better forget that he is educated. Both had much better act as intelligent people—which they are—and work together, to get the job done. This book tries to help with such efforts.

Before getting on with things I have one further suggestion for managers. It has to do with the fads that are certainly as common in the managerial field as anywhere else—possibly even more so. They are often very difficult to distinguish. A "new in thing" hits the field and everyone must soon have one; if they don't, they're not "with it." I suggest that the application of common sense is urgently necessary. For example, the big rush a few years ago to get a computer! Everyone had to have one. After all, our competitors (either government agencies, or businesses) are getting one, we don't want to be left behind. And so, any number of reputable organizations went out and, at very high cost, bought a cannon to shoot a sparrow, so to speak. Many agencies and businesses came to regret bitterly what turned out to be a most unwise investment, at least in terms of the uses planned. We have been treated to the spectacle of companies and agencies taking in each others' washing to keep their various computers fed. The worst part of it all is that for certain purposes the computer is the most wonderful invention of our times. Making a fad out of it nearly resulted in seriously damaging the reputation of one of the finest pieces of equipment now available to us, *when it is used for its real purpose.*

Here, as with other fads and styles, managers are well advised to take it easy and apply large doses of common sense. Investigation before buying is a pretty good watchword. In my own experience with training sessions claimed to have very special results, I have often found it useful to send one or two people to test their value. They were sent not so much to be trained as to evaluate the session. Repeatedly, if you send a person who characteristically renders pretty calm and careful judgments, you won't jump in needlessly. Nevertheless, keep your eyes and ears open for new ideas.

Another valuable procedure concerns office equipment. In my own highly decentralized organization (numbering about 16,000 people) we had a man who happened to be in charge of our communications system. We gave him the additional job of being a specialist on every kind of office equipment—dictating machines, reproduction machines, typewriters, files, and all sorts of other office equipment. He was expected to keep on top of new office devices of every sort—and he did. All salesmen were sent to him and given every opportunity to display their wares— in our central office. Our specialist would invite staff experts in various fields to come by and have a look. We didn't buy too much, but when we did, it was with our eyes open, after a close, careful, and commonsense cost analysis and comparison with costs of existing devices. Incidentally, our communications man made considerable use of the services and wisdom of experienced secretaries. Pretty simple and quite obvious, if you like, but common sense.

From about 1960 I conducted a management seminar in the United States Department of Agriculture Graduate School. This was an advanced class, and it attracted managers from many kinds of organizations in business, industry, and government. There was a wide variety of experience present over the years, and on the whole the groups were a pretty ruthless lot. Some of my loveliest ideas went glimmering before the pragmatism of their attack. Ideas, approaches, systems, books, articles, the presentation of occasional speakers we had—all were very thoroughly considered, evaluated, chewed up, and often ground up into fine bits.

The students (all of them mature adults, and most of them backed by considerable experience) had no particular standards in mind, at least as we ordinarily think of academic standards. I was supposed to be the instructor of these unruly students, but I must confess I learned as much as did any of them, possibly more. Their penetrating questions about ideas and systems boiled down to about four:

1. Do they *work*? And if so, in what setting?
2. Are they *really* efficient?
3. Have they been *proven* successful?
4. Do they make use of the *best* we know about human behavior?

Most of the material in this book went through this seminar, and passed the four questions.

We go now to the ideas that passed . . .

1

About Organizations

ALMOST EVERYONE who works does so in an organization of some size. It may be a business or an industry, or it may be a government agency, a professional association, an educational or religious institution, or some other kind of organization. But whatever its size or kind, an organization consists of people working together to get a job done.

Nobody *owns* an organization. It is possible to own the buildings in which the people work, and the tools, equipment, supplies, and materials they use. But no one owns the people. Each person in an organization can leave it if he wants to.

An organization has often been described as the environment or setting in which people work. What that environment is depends upon what the decision-makers want it to be. The purpose of the organization and its operating policies are ordinarily set by the people who control it. In this environment the people composing the organization perform their work.

In recent years considerable attention has focused on the relation between man and his environment, particularly the so-called natural environment. We have created smog in our atmosphere, filled our clean rivers and lakes with chemical and biological pollutants, ruined lands by unwise cultural methods, and in dozens of other ways made our environment increasingly dirty, ugly, and unpleasant. Numerous, badly needed programs are now under way, aimed at correcting the many mistakes we have made in dealing with the natural environment in which we live. The science of ecology, dealing with interrelationships of man and his environment, has been of great value in developing and carrying out such programs.

I am not intending to suggest that all managers have to study ecology. But there is an interesting and quite practical parallel here. Managers *do* need to consider the relationships between workers and their environment, that is, the organizations in which they work. If anything is clear from innumerable, recent scientific studies, it is that the people who make up an organization react in quite predictable ways to the kind of environment provided by their organization.

An organization fouled with excessive paperwork, red tape, and cumbersome and unnecessary procedures is a poor environment for people; this is obvious. But we foul our organizational environment in more subtle—and often much worse—ways. Unskilled managerial practice, inept supervision, and unfair or harmful personnel policies and practice are examples. Even more subtle are policies or actions that effectively block the many job satisfactions people must have if they are to work with real interest, enthusiasm, and high productivity.

Correction of these mistakes is not always simple or easy. In ecological work with our natural environment, we carefully study all the interrelationships involved. We search for causes and ramifying effects. Then we judiciously eliminate what is causing trouble, aware that such changes will always create still new relationships, and that no change should be made that causes more serious problems than those it solves.

The same kind of thing can take place in an organizational environment. We attempt to do what will most likely improve the organization. But if this is all we do, we are likely to make some serious mistakes. Actually, managers are often so intent on achieving increased profits or additional productivity that they forget or overlook the needs of the people who *are* the organization. Actions aimed at improving an organization will also affect the people in it, and no action should be taken unless both kinds of effects are understood beforehand.

We can pursue these ideas further by noting that an organization has a variety of needs. These include an objective or purpose, a structure with clearcut assignment of duties, good communications, a career system attractive to able people, a management system, efficient production, accurate reporting of results, and so on. At the same time, the individuals in the organization also have some needs. These include some of the same things an organization needs, but also some others—for example, salaries comparable to those paid by other organizations for similar work and the opportunity to achieve and to demonstrate ability, for interesting and challenging work, for recognition, and for advancement.

Both the needs of an organization and the needs of the people in it must be satisfied if the organization is to succeed and remain successful. That this is quite possible has been demonstrated in the business, industrial, and governmental world.

THE ADMINISTRATIVE CLIMATE

We need to note one characteristic of an organization that is not easy to measure, that is often neglected by managing heads, but that every employee knows about. This is the administrative climate.

If the climate is bad, production and morale will be low, while turnover, waste, and union troubles will be high. If the climate is good, turnover, waste, and union troubles will be low, while production and morale will be high.

When we use the term "administrative climate," we have in mind simply the way in which an organization is administered. One example of this has to do with communications. If people know that they can say what they think without fear of reprisal—indeed, if they know that their ideas are really *wanted* by the managers of the organization—then we can say that the administrative climate of the organization is good, as seen by the people in it. Conversely, if the people know that they had better not say what they really think because if they do, they risk losing their jobs; if they know their ideas are *not* wanted, that all they are supposed to do is work at their assigned tasks, and that no one really cares what they think about it—then the climate is bad.

Where it is unsafe or unwise for anyone to say what he really thinks about the work of the organization, no amount of training in communications will bring about an improvement in communications. Where supervisors are expected by the managing officials of an organization to be tough drivers, the kind of people who will "stand for no nonsense," supervisory training is a waste. Where people know from experience that the suggestion system does not work because basically the managing officials really do not want any ideas from subordinates, campaigns using the full paraphernalia of suggestion boxes, certificates, and cash awards are bound to fail.

A great many evaluations of supervisory training have shown conclusively that successful supervision cannot be conducted in an unfavorable environment. You can take first-line supervisors out of their organization, for example, and subject them to the best course in supervisory training that can be developed, but you cannot assume that they can return to their organization and practice what they have learned in school. This is simply because supervisors with even just a few years of experience are products of the organizations in which they work. Trained and developed as better, more skillful, more knowledgeable supervisors, they return home to find things exactly as they were when they left.

The new skills do not necessarily work in the old setting. The setting itself may have to change to accommodate the new breed of supervisor.

I am not overdrawing this point. If you train someone you must train them appropriately for the situation in which they will be working. A great many companies and many government agencies have discovered this. Some have not. Certainly the supervisors who get the training will confirm this. Among the thousands of supervisors I have dealt with in courses, conferences, workshops, and by correspondence, there is a common complaint: "This is great stuff that I have learned, but how can I hope to use it in *my* organization when I get home?" Frequently they add feelingly, "My boss will never go for this!"

And here we have a major problem. If we really want improved supervision, then we must at the same time improve the climate, the setting, the environment—that is, the organization—in which our trained supervisors can work. It is only half a solution to train supervisors, leaving the environment unchanged. Indeed, it is less than half a solution, since the trained supervisor cannot really operate.

What I am saying is that the efforts being made by all kinds of organizations to improve their supervision are bound to fail unless equal attention is given to an environment in which modern supervision can be practiced. It will be worthwhile here to examine the characteristics of truly modern organizations. The fact is that a knowledge explosion has taken place, not only in the physical sciences, but in the biological and human behavioral sciences as well. There is new knowledge about organizations.

CLIMATE INDICATORS

There are a number of ways we can tell whether the administrative climate in an organization is a good one. Many organizations may not have correct or complete information on some points, but this can be remedied, as we shall see. At any rate, our first indicator or barometer is:

1. Turnover

Turnover, as determined by the U. S. Bureau of Labor Statistics, and as used widely by management experts, is expressed in a *monthly* percentage figure. Thus, if an organization has a turnover of 5 percent, this means that 5 people in every 100 are leaving each month. The turnover percentages are not used to express the number of people per hundred leaving in a year. To make this crystal clear, a 1,000-man organization with a steady 5 percent turnover is losing 50 people each month. In a year this organization will lose upwards of 600 people, if the turnover keeps going at the same rate. Obviously, any organization would be seriously affected by a turnover of this magnitude.

The effects of turnover are fairly obvious and should be well known. Recruitment must increase as the turnover percentage increases, if the organization hopes to stay in business. Training of the new recruits must increase at an equally rapid rate. Losses in production (of whatever the organization produces) are involved, since these losses also increase with turnover. In total, the effects of a high turnover rate are quite serious, with the possible exception of one factor that many people claim to be beneficial. This factor is that "new blood" is being fed into the organization. However, this beneficial effect can be overdone, as we shall see later.

A turnover rate of 4.2 percent will remove about half the organization annually. Thus, in a 1,000-person organization, 42 people will leave per month. Multiplied by 12 months, the figure becomes 504, or about half the total number of 1,000. But such a conclusion is not quite valid since several people may enter and leave the same job in a single year.

A real question now arises: What is a *low* turnover? This

question cannot be answered with certainty. The lowest turnover on record of a sizable organization has been maintained by Lincoln Electric of Cleveland for a number of years. The rate is an impressive 0.33 percent. The figure means that one person in a hundred is leaving each 3 months, or that 4 out of 100 leave in a year. The U. S. Soil Conservation Service, a federal government agency of about 15,000 people, has maintained a turnover rate of 0.4 to 0.5 percent for more than 18 years. This is probably the lowest rate in the federal government. Both these organizations have been highly successful over long periods. But in both organizations the managing heads have kept a careful eye on the monthly turnover rate and moved into action if it went up. In other words, neither of these low rates is accidental.

Some managers may delude themselves with their own figures. One manager in a scientific institution was quite satisfied with the "low" turnover among his professional people. However, the turnover in technicians, clerks, typists, secretarial help, and other nonprofessionals in his organization was very high. When this was called to his attention, he snorted, "These people don't count; they're not trained professionals." This manager was about two-thirds correct; one-third of the people in his organization were subprofessionals, but they were there to make it possible for the professionals to work at their greatest capacity. The high costs of turnover were there, but the manager couldn't see them.

This points to the need for collection of the correct figures. If the figures include people who are *not* leaving voluntarily—as for retirement—they may hide indications important to know about. It is the so-called "quit rate" for the total organization the manager needs to have.

Table 1 shows what turnover rates mean in three organizations of increasingly larger size. Turnover in organizations larger than this can readily be calculated. For example, an organization with 100,000 people will lose 10 times as many people both monthly and annually as the organization with 10,000—at the various rates shown.

TABLE 1

Turnover Rates

Size of Organization	Monthly Percent	Monthly Losses	Annual Losses
1,000 employees	0.1	1	12
	0.2	2	24
	0.3	3	36
	0.4	4	48
	0.5	5	60
	1.0	10	120
	2.0	20	240
	3.0	30	360
10,000 employees	0.1	10	120
	0.2	20	240
	0.3	30	360
	0.4	40	480
	0.5	50	600
	1.0	100	1,200
	2.0	200	2,400
	3.0	300	3,600
20,000 employees	0.1	20	240
	0.2	40	480
	0.3	60	720
	0.4	80	960
	0.5	100	1,200
	1.0	200	2,400
	2.0	400	4,800
	3.0	600	7,200

In reviewing turnover rates in business, industrial, and government organizations, it is by no means uncommon to find rates that range from 2 to 5 percent. Rates higher than this are less common, but they do occasionally occur. Managers would do well to assemble and keep an eye on turnover figures. In times when jobs are easy to get, high rates usually indicate something wrong with the organization. Low rates indicate that people want to stay put, and that the climate of the company or agency is in good shape, as far as they are concerned.

It should also be noted that *where* the turnover occurs is important to know as well. There will be differences among branch, regional, or area offices, and among different kinds of workers. For example, somewhat higher rates are often encountered with women workers who leave to get married or to have children. Where differences occur between branch offices, there is always the possibility that the man in charge is responsible. This should be carefully evaluated. There may, of course, be other reasons.

It is noticeable too that turnover is frequently higher among lower-paid workers. Managers may conclude from this, without assembling the facts available, that this is because of competition from other companies or agencies. They pay more, so the story goes, and so we lose people to them. But several questions arise here:

- If other organizations pay more, why can't we? Do they, in fact, really pay more?
- Is it really higher pay, or are there other factors? Maybe the administrative climate is better elsewhere.
- What are the costs in dollars and cents of the higher turnover among low-paid workers? Could this amount—or anything less than this amount—be spent on actions that would hold the experienced workers?
- Are unions particularly active among lower-paid workers? If they are, this may be a dead giveaway that there is employee dissatisfaction and that the organization might profitably be able to correct this.

Such questions as these simply cannot be answered by a manager off the top of his head. Experience is not always safe to rely upon either, since conditions have a way of changing. Correct answers require careful study to ascertain the real facts of the matter. Once the facts—not opinions—are available, then more enlightened decisions can be made.

As with various other statistical reports, turnover figures do not, in themselves, tell what is the matter. They only indicate that employees are leaving at a certain rate. If the rate of quitting is much beyond, say, 0.5 percent, and for no apparent reason, the next step would seem to be obvious: find the reason. Here again, it is unwise to rely too heavily on experience. The manager should have data collected that will tell him *without doubt* why the rate is higher than normal or desirable.

THE COSTS OF TURNOVER

Because turnover or quit rates are usually expressed on a monthly percentage basis, their apparently small size often leads to feelings of security when they should lead to the reverse. Offhand, a 1 percent turnover sounds pretty small. However, as Table 1 shows, this amounts to hundreds of people leaving annually from a smaller organization, or thousands from a larger one.

Actually there is a simple way of estimating the costs of turnover. It works like this:

Assuming a 1 percent turnover in a 10,000-man organization, and assuming that positions or jobs must be filled as each person leaves, then the cost of turnover equals:

(1) The amounts spent on recruitment of new people, including planning, preparation of brochures, advertising, interviewing, selection, and the like;

(2) Plus the production losses sustained (in *any* way) because an experienced employee disappeared, and therefore did not produce;

(3) Plus all the costs of training a new employee up to full production. As a quick, rough approximation, suppose it takes about a year, on the average, to get a new employee fully into production. If the average salary amounts to, say, $6,000 a year, the cost of training can be shown to be about $3,000.

In Figure 1, everything *above* the diagonal line is shown as no production since the employee cannot produce until he has

Figure 1

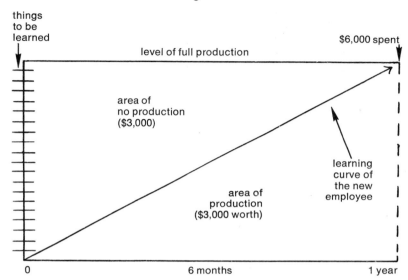

things
to be
learned

level of full production

$6,000 spent

area of
no production
($3,000)

learning
curve of
the new
employee

area of
production
($3,000 worth)

0   6 months   1 year

learned. Once he has learned what he must do then he can produce—as shown by the area *under* the diagonal line.

Applying this idea to our mythical organization: A 1 percent turnover per month for 10,000 employees amounts to 100 people per month or 1,200 per year. Multiplying 1,200 by $3,000 gives us $3,600,000. This is the loss sustained because new employees can't produce from scratch, but must learn how first.

As we have already noted, turnover figures of 2 to 5 percent are common enough in many organizations. If the organization is a large one, the training costs become astronomical. Thus, in an organization of 500,000 people (again assuming a $6,000 entrance salary and a training time of about a year), the cost of learning amounts to $15,000,000 with a 1 percent turnover, or $30,000,000 with 2 percent, or $75,000,000 with 5 percent.

When costs of recruitment are added to these figures, the costs go still higher. These vary, of course, by geographic area, scarcity or abundance of recruits, how long it takes to find a qualified person, how elaborate the activity is, and so on. Losses in production depend on what is being produced and what happened when an employee left. If other employees picked up the load, what happened to *their* regular work, and how much did this cost the organization? Chances are the training losses may be doubled by such additions. If so, the losses will be doubled.

For the rather obvious reasons shown above, in cash costs alone, to say nothing of other adjustments impossible to calculate in dollars, it seems clear that turnover rates deserve close attention. But there is still another reason why these rates are important to a manager:

The brighter students leaving high school, business school, or college are usually aware that high turnover rates indicate unsatisfactory working conditions, that is to say, poor management. Other things being equal, they will go with the organization with the lowest turnover. Thus, the rate of turnover may actually affect the ability of an organization to attract the best qualified people. This is by no means the only factor a prospective employee may consider, but it can, and it sometimes does, play a critical role.

2. *Amount of Waste or Red Tape*

A second indicator of good administrative climate is the amount of waste or red tape.

If the people of an organization want it to succeed as much as its managers do, then they will do everything they can to eliminate waste, duplication, overlapping, and red tape. This has been shown to be true in a great many successful organizations. The reverse has been found in poor organizations floundering along in a rut leading to failure.

There is a mistaken belief that employees will not act to correct wasteful practices unless they are rewarded or paid for doing so. To a certain extent this is true, as some companies have found after installing a bonus system of some kind. On the other hand, cash alone is not the sole answer. There are many examples of government agencies where bonuses cannot be used and cash awards are quite low, and still wasteful practices are overcome by the employees themselves without urging by management. The employees are rewarded, all right, but not with cash. These ideas derive from studies made by Likert, Herzberg, and numerous other studies on the factors that motivate people.

Methods for detecting and eliminating waste, red tape, cumbersome procedures, and outdated methods are considered later on. Here we may note that the experts most likely to be of help in uncovering inefficiencies are the people who are doing the work. They usually know where the trouble spots are and can ordinarily offer very practical suggestions for their elimination. The manager's problem is to gain the enthusiastic cooperation of these employees.

3. Productivity and Its Cost

In a good climate, the cost of the product (whether something manufactured or a service provided) is going down, is maintained at a steady low level, or if going up, it is going up more slowly than the costs of input.

This can be stated in another way: In a good climate, productivity per man or man-hour is going up, is maintained at a high level, or if going down, the reasons for the decline are beyond the workers' control.

These facts are not difficult to ascertain. Declining productivity or increasing costs are easy enough to measure. But the tacit assumption that rising costs of material or input is the only reason may not be the correct answer. If turnover is high, union troubles many, or waste common, then the rising costs and lower productivity are almost certainly related to a poor administrative climate. This may be, usually is, a more important factor than rising costs of input. It was no accident that cost of product dropped 20 percent in 30 years while costs of labor and materials rose from 300 to more than 500 percent at Lincoln Electric in Cleveland. This had to do, as Lincoln himself noted, with the participation of the people making up the company; that is, with people working in an excellent administrative climate.

4. Employee Attitudes and Feelings About Organization

If the attitude of the employees is strongly favorable the climate is far better than if it is strongly unfavorable or indifferent.

This indicator is much more difficult to get at than others which can be measured in more concrete terms. Various behavioral scientists have devised tests and questionnaires to ascertain employee attitudes. These are not too easy to devise, and they can be somewhat tricky to use. Well handled, however, such evaluations of employee attitudes can be invaluable.

The way we get at the problem of integrating people and their organizations is by considering the question: What do people want from their jobs? In the same breath perhaps, we need also to consider the reverse question: What do people *not* want from their jobs?

If we have clear answers to offer, with respect to people's wants or needs, then we are in a position to construct an organization responsive to those needs. If this organization can be constructed so as to be able to succeed as an organization, then our integration can be complete.

Incidentally, what *is* a successful organization? If it is an industrial organization, it must produce a quality product at a competitive price, thereby producing a sure profit. If it is a business, it must so choose its ventures and so perform its operation as to be competitive, thereby producing a profit. If it is a government agency, it must so conduct its operations as to provide a maximum of quality service at a minimum cost, thereby justifying its existence to taxpayers. Many other criteria can be used, but in the final analysis, a successful organization is one that provides a product or a service of sufficient value to both stockholders and customers to keep it operating. (The stockholders in a government agency are the taxpayers, who are also the customers.) We will return to this idea later when we have considered peoples wants and needs in relation to an organization—any organization.

2

A System of Career Development

THE BEST recent research results available indicate that an organization is likely to be successful in proportion to the fullest continuing efforts of all the people who compose it. All things being equal, interested, enthusiastic, productive people who want an organization to succeed can almost guarantee its success. Conversely, indifferent, even apathetic people, most of whom are simply in their jobs to earn a living, can almost guarantee ultimate failure of the organization.

In any career system, the central idea is to enable people to pursue lifelong careers in the organization, dependent of course on the excellence of their performance. Any practice or custom that tends to impair the efforts or injure the development of the people of an organization tends to diminish the possibility of that organization's success. The managing heads of a business or industry, of a government agency, or of other institutions need to understand the value of the human beings that *are* the organization they command. If they can do this, if they can perceive their organization in this way, then it should follow that they will develop policies and take those actions most likely to enable their people to produce with excellence to their fullest possible capacity. There is no implication here that a career system is intended primarily to produce happy, contented people. This is nonsense. In the best career systems that have been studied, the people are not all necessarily satisfied and completely happy. In fact, they may be dissatisfied in the sense that they are anxious to do much better than they have so far been able to do. A striving for greater achievement is not necessarily comfortable. Imaginative, innovative thinking is not necessarily easy; it is often very hard work. Satisfaction may be a byproduct of an individual's progress, but it is not an end in itself.

THE POTENTIAL-DEVELOPING ENVIRONMENT

The intent of a career development system is to provide the environment and the incentives that will help the people of the organization to achieve to their fullest potential. In a general way such an environment is characterized by the following:

1. Continuing, Uninterrupted Employment

You cannot carry on a career program if it is marked at intervals by disaster, and an interruption in employment is, of course, such a disaster. Layoffs in industry and reductions-in-force in government are first-class deterrents to career programs, and in the past they seem to have been the usual thing rather than the exception. In industry, people may be laid off when a slump occurs, when a change in equipment is necessary, or for various other reasons. In government, the vagaries of appropriation bodies may seem to require layoffs, or as the government calls these, reductions-in-force. They may also occur because an agency wishes to change its organization in some way—usually explained as an attempt to increase efficiency of operation.

Actually, both industrial layoffs and government reductions-in-force take place for the most part because managing officials do not plan to avoid them. It takes farsighted planning to provide continuing employment, and such planning must provide for financial reserves of a sort appropriate to the organization which can be drawn upon in case of necessity.

Specifically, in government, there are three obvious, even if little-used, ways to do this:

The first is to develop financial plans that take fully and correctly into account the turnover in personnel that always occurs in every agency. Personnel and budget officers cooperating can forecast turnover on the basis of recent experience, both in numbers of people and dollars.

The second is to identify work that is best performed by temporary people who do not wish to join the agency for a career, but who work only on a parttime basis as one way of supplementing their income. Any necessary budget reductions then result simply in not employing temporary people until turnover makes possible the resumption of normal or reduced activity. But the solid corps of permanent, career personnel is not touched. The percentage of personnel funds used for permanent and for temporary people can be based on experience with previous budget cuts. For temporaries 10 percent is a fairly realistic figure, but this must be adjusted to fit the organization's actual experience.

The third measure is to purchase equipment on a planned basis so that in the event of retrenchment, equipment purchasing can safely be deferred until it is possible to balance the budget. In this situation we take the cut in equipment rather than in people. This means that we use equipment just a little longer before replacement. If the equipment-replacement program is kept up to date, this should almost always be possible.

Other means suggest themselves, such as deferring travel, reducing the number of conferences, and otherwise tightening up on activities. What these means are depends upon the organization and the kind of work it performs. But all this is developed to avoid cutting into the organization—that is, the career people—on a panic basis.

It is appropriate to note at this point that when a government agency or a major segment of it is wiped out by legislative or executive action, then the preceding measures have little bearing. Fortunately, this situation is relatively rare. Similarly, the suggested measures would have little value in an industry which loses a large government contract after a period during which contracts were relatively continuous.

Measures similar to the three suggested above have been successfully used in industrial concerns. Here, as in government, the prime requisites are a clear understanding of the need for continuous employment and a real desire to achieve it. An outstanding and remarkably successful example of this is to be found in the Lincoln Electric Company of Cleveland.[1]

The founder of that company makes an important point: that during a slow business period, industries don't tear down part of their plants or sell off their machine tools. Nor do they lay off their presidents, their officers, their superintendents, or their experts. Instead they lay off the employees who do the work and who are least able to stand the loss of income. The layoff policy results in tremendous costs due to the workers' attitude about efficiency. "No worker," notes Lincoln, "will strive for efficient production when his very efficiency will throw him out on the street that much sooner, and no sane man would expect him to do so."

This company has successfully used for a half century a series of measures aimed at providing continuous employment, even during slack periods:

1. Fully explained and documented in *A New Approach to Industrial Economics*, by James F. Lincoln. New York: Devin-Adair Co., 1961.

- Manufacture to stock.
- Develop new machines and methods that have been noted or indicated during active times. Slack times provide the workers and the time for experimentation.
- Reduce prices by getting lower costs. In slack times, work with the workers to find new ways.
- Explore new markets that may have been passed over when times were good.
- Develop new products.
- If worse comes to worst, reduce hours of work, *if the employees are willing and agreeable.*

By such means as these it was possible for the Lincoln Electric Company—the world's largest manufacturer of arc-welding equipment—to report no necessity for layoffs when business slumped. And the turnover rate, by the way, has for years been 5 to 10 times lower at Lincoln Electric than for all heavy industry.

2. Turnover Properly Related to Stability

The second environmental factor of importance is turnover properly related to stability. The word turnover is used here to mean the number of people who leave an organization in relation to the total number of people the organization contains. It is figured conveniently on a monthly basis, and is expressed as a percentage. For example, if an average of 3 people in 100 leave an organization each month, this is expressed as a turnover rate of 3 percent. If the turnover were 1 percent, this would mean that 1 person in 100 was leaving each month.

People may leave for a variety of reasons—to take jobs in other places, to start their own business, or whatever. All this is counted. What the manager needs to know is what the actual turnover rate is, because it may indicate any of a number of things. Obviously, he must also search out the reasons why people are leaving.

A high turnover rate in good times may mean that something is wrong with the organization, that the people don't like it for some reason. Or it may mean—and this is almost the same thing—that with good times, other opportunities appear more attractive. The rate itself, however, does not reveal the reason why people are leaving; it merely shows that they are. The reason needs to be uncovered, since high turnover is a costly loss to any organization.

If the high turnover occurs in bad times, then there is every likelihood that something is indeed wrong with the organization. People ordinarily don't leave jobs in bad times, for the obvious reason that employment is hard to get. When they do, an organization had better look to its policies and administrative climate.

Low turnover rates in almost any organization may mean that people like the work and the organization, especially in good times. In bad times, low rates may mean only that people are simply holding on to the jobs they have. In either case—high rates or low—there are several points to bear in mind:

■ The first is that *some* personnel turnover may be a good thing. It provides leeway for adjustments that may be needed in the structure and staffing of the organization. It makes possible a steady flow of new people into an organization. This flow may be of vital importance. It brings to bear the contribution of new minds, and it may help to introduce new vigor and enthusiasm.

■ Turnover rates should be closely watched, not only for the organization as a whole, but also for the various important segments of it. Such rates are key indicators to well-informed managers, indicators that may well call for action.

■ Turnover rates are profitably used in planning changes that may affect the number of jobs either in the whole organization or in parts of it. For example, if a contemplated reorganization will eliminate, say, 300 jobs, and the going turnover rate is 100 a month, then within three or four months the changes can usually be effected without laying off anyone. This of course presumes that the organization has put itself in a position to retrain and place people in other jobs. In the federal government this should be quite easy to do because of the large size of that organization, although the necessary machinery to do it has never been perfected. Reductions commonly are going on in one agency while hiring is going on in another. Large industries should be able to handle retraining and placement if they have set up the means to do so. Smaller concerns might find it less easy, but then the layoffs in smaller businesses are necessarily smaller, so that percentage-wise the principle may still apply.

The biggest barrier to this kind of approach to reorganization or adjustment is the attitude of managing officials. If they are indifferent or inept, then there is little likelihood that continuous employment will be planned for. We need to remember at this point that there are numerous examples of highly successful business, industrial, and government organizations that have brought off such changes over periods of many decades without layoffs or forced reductions. What this seems to mean is that where there's a will, a way can be found.

3. Good Participative Climate

A good participative climate is the third of the environmental factors of importance. It involves two ideas that are very closely related. The first is that all the people in an organization must feel free to speak their minds without fear of any kind of reprisal. More important is the second idea: that the ideas of all the people in an organization must be sought, and that they thereby have a voice in running the organization.

The common point of these two ideas is that the active participation of all the people in an organization must be enlisted, encouraged, and arranged for with respect to the development and operation of all those policies and procedures that affect the work done. The administrative climate cannot appear to be no more than permissive, or appear merely to tolerate indulgently the participation of people. Rather, it must be such that people understand their contribution of ideas to be sincerely desired and eagerly sought. Managers and supervisors must convince the people at every turn that their contributions are *wanted*.

I am aware that this idea of employee participation has been publicly and often bitterly debated for many years. However, the weight of evidence in its favor is far too great to make further argument useful. Not only do we have the results of scientific research by sociologists and psychologists; we are also able to review numerous outstanding and practical examples of companies, businesses, and government agencies where the principle of participation has been hugely successful for many years.[2]

Possibly the best summary statement of the matter was made by E. Wight Bakke,[3] director of the Yale University Labor and Management Center, who said:

". . . self-realization in our culture is intimately bound up with the degree to which people are able to participate, under intelligent and rational leadership, and the degree to which they have an effective voice in determining the rules and conditions under which, and the plans according to which, they live and work."

There are many ways by means of which people composing an organization may participate in helping to run it. Formal machinery can be set up, such as employee councils, employee advisory boards, suggestion systems, and the like. But there is little doubt that possibly the best means of all is the development of an understanding by every supervisor of the value of participation and the high productive potential of the combined minds of all his people.

2. The interested reader is referred to the writings of Kurt Lewin, Rensis Likert, E. Wight Bakke, Burleigh Gardner, Joseph Scanlon, Alexander Leighton, Robert Morton, Alex Bavelas, Elton Mayo, Alfred Marrow, F. J. Roethlisberger, and Douglas McGregor, among others.
3. "The Function of Management," in *Human Relations and Modern Management*, ed. E. M. Hugh-Jones (Amsterdam: North Holland Publishing Co., 1958), pp. 241–42. See also *The Successful Supervisor* by the author (3rd ed., New York: Harper & Row Publishers, Inc., 1974; pp. 46–61).

4. Equivalent Compensation

Equivalent compensation is a fourth environmental factor important in a career program. It is quite obvious, but it must not be overlooked. This is one area, incidentally, where "keeping up with the Joneses" has a certain real importance.

The general principle here is that compensation for work performed in one organization should be approximately equal to the compensation for similar work in other organizations. This idea is easy enough to state; it applies with particular force where there is competition for people. But it is by no means easy to apply.

We cannot consider compensation as simply the wages or salary paid. We could do that many years ago but not at the present time. As viewed these days, compensation includes quite a variety of things, some of them tangible, some not. The list might include such things as these:

Salary or wages
Bonuses
Paid leave or vacations
Health and life insurance benefits
Retirement benefits
Career possibilities or promotion opportunities
Fair personnel policies and practices
Suitable working facilities and equipment
Enlightened supervision
Strong training programs
Interesting, challenging work

Such a list could be much expanded to include all those things people like about an organization. Many of the items have been dubbed "fringe benefits," but there is really nothing fringe about them. Some have come about after bitter fights between unions and management; some have been legislated into being by Congress. But they all form part of the compensation for working.

One or several of these items may be better in one organization, or they may not be as good. The precise order of their importance is not surely known at the present time, although we are learning something about their priority from various studies.[4] We are also learning that some factors are more important than others, depending on whether the worker is unskilled, skilled, subprofessional, professional, male or female.

In any event, it seems clear that any organization must give thoughtful attention to all its kinds of compensation. They will affect the organization's administrative climate, its turnover, the quality of the people it can recruit, and ultimately, its success.

ELEMENTS OF A CAREER SYSTEM

Given continuous employment, a low turnover, a good participative climate, and equality of compensation, an organization can then hope to develop a system of career development that can be successful. There are many practical operating methods to be considered, but for our purposes we can best describe the more important principles or ideas that have proven most useful in systems that have been operating for many years.

1. Recruitment and Selection

Recruitment and selection must result in well-qualified people joining the organization. This applies primarily to the beginning positions, but to a certain extent it may apply to higher positions as well.

To start with, recruiting efforts need to be *honest*. If we hold out glittering possibilities that fail of fulfillment, our public image will become tarnished very quickly. We dare not make

4. See *Motivation to Work* by Frederick Herzberg, Bernard Mausner, and B. B. Snyderman (New York: John Wiley & Sons, 1959; 2nd ed.). Also *Work and the Nature of Man* by F. Herzberg (New York: World Publishing Co., 1966).

promises or implied promises when we are uncertain whether they can be made good. We need to approach the recruitment of new people, not as salesmen, but as consultants.

The selections we make are difficult because no one is really expert in judging people and their potential. The psychologists have worked hard at devising tests that may tell us how able or how skilled a human being may be in performing various types of work. This kind of testing deserves every possible encouragement; we certainly ought to know more about how to evaluate human beings. But the entire subject of testing has been undergoing considerable argument and debate, even among the psychologists. Our experts are by no means agreed on how conclusive the various tests actually are. In all conscience, it would seem wise to use such tests with moderation, and to consider them in relation to the best judgment we are capable of rendering.

We need to observe and question, to discuss and probe, to review previous experience and education. We need to be critically aware of the need for objectivity in our evaluations. Above all, we need to remember that no one person is really expert, and that it had probably best be a group of people that render judgment about a human being rather than a single individual.

It has seemed to me for many years that a device used by the federal government in the employment of new people has much to recommend it. When a person applies for work under the Civil Service system of the government, he must pass a test—either an actual examination, or a listing of his qualifications, or both. He is then rated and put on a list in the order in which he will be given consideration when vacancies occur. When he is selected by an agency, he goes to work, but he is not yet accepted as a full-fledged employee. Instead, for a full year, he is on trial. This is known as his probationary or trial period. It is not generally realized, even in the government service, that this period is a continuation of his test—a further testing, if you will.

During the employee's probationary or trial period he is supposed to be "tested" by every practical means. His supervisor is expected to proceed vigorously with his training, to try him in as many kinds of situations as possible, to observe his reactions and performance, and finally, to recommend whether to give him permanent status or let him go. What this means is that a new employee is tested in his job for up to a full year before he is accepted. The fact that some government supervisors fail to take correct and full advantage of this test period, and hence poor employees are sometimes given permanent status, is beside the point.

This testing mechanism is a very valuable one; it is of great help in making sound selections. As used by skilled supervisors, it is about as good a means as has been devised for judging the qualities of new recruits. After all, close study of a man performing in his job for a year can tell a great deal about his present and future worth as a career employee. It can also help the employee to decide whether he is in the organization that he *wants* to be in.

2. Placement

Placement of people must result in a good "fit" between an individual and his job. Constant observation of his performance on the job can tell us whether this is true, provided there is a perceptive supervisor to make the necessary observations.

Placement is not a one-time matter. People need to be constantly observed to ascertain which aspects of their jobs interest them most, and which are uninteresting. Placement, in fact, must go on all the way through an employee's career as we observe strong and weak capabilities.

3. Training

We have considered the subject of training and training systems elsewhere. Here we may simply summarize that training is primarily a supervisory function and responsibility. It should be planned and executed systematically and in close parallel with the career development of individual people. It is a most important component of any career system. And, it is expensive, and therefore should be performed with all possible efficiency.

4. Promotion

The promotion of an individual is always something of a gamble. When we give a person additional responsibility, broader functions, and new work to do, we are, in effect, betting that his performance will confirm our judgment. We put money on this bet—in the increased salary and other compensations he will get in the new position.

Everyone knows, of course, that an experienced gambler tries to reduce the element of chance as much as he can in order to be that much more certain of winning his bet. This is also what we do when we promote someone—that is, we try to be as sure as we can, ahead of time, that our bet in promoting an employee will pay off.

A number of people in our society are quite confident of their ability to pick a winner. Watching them perform, say at the racetrack, can be amusing. But their guesses, both right and wrong, are not so amusing when they concern people. The fact is that no single person has ever been able to pick infallibly winners among people. I have watched many executives who claim they could always spot a good person after they had known him a little while—sometimes a very little while indeed. Such supremely confident judges of people make plenty of mistakes in judgment, but they will rationalize this by noting that this or that man "let me down." What let them down, in fact, was their own judgment.

Psychological and other tests have not proven perfect either. It is not enough to know that a test will be right 85 percent of the time—not when human careers and lives are at stake. By all means we need to use suitable tests to help reduce chance, but certainly as of now we cannot rely absolutely on them. The tests cannot do the job for us. Judgment must still come into play in the final decision.

What this brings us to is the idea that promotions should involve:

- Reduction of chance by *recorded trials* in work that is parallel or comparable to the work in the position to be filled.
- *Multiple opinions* from several people qualified to judge because of their familiarity with the person's work, preferably over a reasonable period of time.
- *Interviews* with the candidates for promotion.
- Training of the promoted individual.

In the end, some one manager must decide who is to be promoted, but he is well advised to consider these points before he does so. In gambler's terms this is known as hedging your bet, and it makes gambling somewhat less likely to result in serious losses.

Recorded Trials: A supervisory principle known as the developmental or career principle states: People should have opportunities to show that they can accept greater responsibility.[5] Experienced supervisors create these opportunities so that they may be able to observe performance under increased responsibility. Organizations need to encourage use of this principle by all supervisors, and to require the development and maintenance of appropriate records about observed performance. This is scarcely a burden. All it takes is a memo or note to the individual's personnel file showing what opportunity he was given and how well he did in discharging the responsibility. If he flubbed it, the supervisor need make no note for the file; rather, he tries the individual again after a little more coaching or training.

Careful records of this sort, accumulated over the years, can be of great value to the manager who must decide upon promotion. Actually such records can express pretty well the progress made by an individual throughout his career. These are, in fact, a great deal more important than most of the usual records stored in personnel files.

---

5. *The Successful Supervisor*, by William R. Van Dersal. New York: Harper & Row Publishers; 3rd ed., 1974, pp. 18–20.

Multiple Opinions: There are two ways to think about the promotion of an individual. You can promote him on the basis of his past performance—as a recognition of his previous good work. Or you can promote him because of his qualifications for the new job. These qualifications are judged on the basis of their showing in the work he has done in the past. Thus, if a man has shown initiative in the job he holds, chances are he will continue to show initiative in the new position.

Often these two approaches to promotion are mixed. An exceptionally good operator in one job may not be the best candidate for a job of greater responsibility. For example, not all patrolmen can perform well as sergeants—who are supervisors —even though some may have been the finest patrolmen on the police force. When promotion has been perceived primarily as recognition for excellent work, many systems have fallen apart. A tiptop scientist is by no means always a tiptop supervisor.

A simple device of value here is an ad hoc form such as Figure 2.

The names in the first column (1) include all the candidates thought to be possibly eligible for a given vacancy. In the series of columns under (2) write in the characteristics needed in the new job. Then place a plus, check, or a minus under each characteristic for each person. A plus means well above average, a check means about average, and a minus means definitely below average.

What we have done here is to make a whole series of smaller judgments about each individual being considered. Multiple judgment is provided for by having several evaluators use such a form. A composite summary can be made later, using red ink for one evaluator, green for another, black for a third, and so on.

When all items are completed and put on the summary form (and note that not every judge will know *all* the characteristics of *every* person), then they can be added and put in the summary column (3). There, we put down so many pluses, so many checks, and so many minuses. Any individual getting all pluses would top the list. Giving numerical ratings to the pluses, checks,

Figure 2

(1) name	(2) Initiative	Adaptability	Technical Know-how	Ability to write	Drive	etc.	etc.	(3) summary
1.								
2.								
3.								
4.								
5.								
6.								

and minuses adds nothing; it may easily hide a serious deficiency.

I have always liked this simple technique. It gets all eligible people into consideration. It brings to light differences in judgment among the judges. And importantly, it is done in the most timely way—that is, when it is most clear what the new job will entail, as seen at the time it is to be filled.

This sort of ranking of candidates can be done in dozens of

other ways. There is nothing particularly scientific about any of them, including the one described. But going through some kind of thoughtful and objective ranking is important. It tends to reduce preconceptions. It helps the manager think things through. It takes a little time, and hence reduces hasty decisions. And it assures all eligible employees of careful consideration. After all, a manager must be sure not only why he picked a particular individual for a job, but also why he did *not* pick each of the other individuals who didn't quite measure up. This latter is important, too, because the ratings may have revealed characteristics of various individuals that can be corrected or improved. This again goes back to the supervisors concerned for action leading to improvement.

Interviews: Given several possible candidates for a vacancy, the decision maker had best have a talk with each one. Unfortunately, this is not always done. It is not too difficult if the candidates are all in the same location. Frequently, however, they are not, especially in organizations spread widely over the country. Nevertheless, despite travel and other costs, a manager should have his talk with each one. It may help him finalize his decision. It may reveal some elements he hadn't thought of. It may uncover one or more candidates who are not interested in the vacancy at all—and perhaps for good reason.

In the interview we seek to learn something about each individual's attitude. Reviewing his present job may reveal real enthusiasm—or lack of it. Considering his ambitions, his opinions of the company or agency, and possibly things he would change if he could—all these may reveal his way of thinking and his attack on problems. Importantly too, is he likely to prove to be a yes-man? What are his opinions about unions? About equal employment for women? About minority groups?

The interview is not simply an opportunity for confirming the written record. Rather it is an opportunity for learning about the candidate's opinions, attitudes, beliefs, ambitions, and hopes. It takes a little doing to get a candidate to divulge all these. But the effort is well worth it. Costs of such interviews are negligible compared to costs that will accrue later if a decision turns out to be wrong. Incidentally, we have been discussing promotion as though the manager himself were going to be the supervisor of the person promoted. We need to note, therefore, that if he is not, then the actual supervisor should be playing a full part in the process. He should judge the candidates as far as he is able, rank them, conduct all or part of the interview. In the end he should be asked for his recommendations, and he should be able to defend them. After all, we're interested in developing supervisors also, and this provides an excellent opportunity. There is always the chance that the manager and the supervisor may not agree, and this must be resolved by the manager. He will do well here to be sure his supervisor understands the reasons he has been overruled if this proves necessary.

Training the Promoted Individual: Once the decision is made and the best candidate selected, two steps are indicated. One is to advise supervisors of candidates who didn't quite make it on points they may want to strengthen. The other is to start—or preferably to complete—the job training of the new incumbent. No matter how high the position or how well qualified the candidate may be, this training is very important. We can scarcely specify what it should be, but it should never be neglected.

5. Retirement

Somehow the subject of retirement is commonly and mistakenly relegated to the closing years of a person's career. And, also commonly, the closer a person is to retirement, the more delicate the subject seems to get. There is a sort of feeling that a man is worn out, tired, or over the hill by the time he is within sight of retiring. This is foolishness. It is somewhat the same as thinking that life insurance is a delicate matter because it implies that the insured may ultimately die. And so will we all. But this doesn't stop us from paying close attention to good insurance plans. Everyone retires, too, sooner or later, if he doesn't die before he gets there, to put it bluntly.

The age of 65 years is presently set as retirement age under Social Security and in many pension plans based partly or wholly on Social Security. The federal government sets 70 years as its mandatory retirement age in most agencies. In certain hazardous work, people may retire earlier, in government and industry.

These fixed points for mandatory retirement have little scientific foundation. They have been shown to result in a switch in objectives of people approaching the mandatory deadline.[6] People switch from getting greatest satisfaction from achievement, challenging work, and greater responsibility to worrying about increasing their pension amounts, enjoying greater status, plush office furnishings, and the like. Their motivation during the last few years changes from the satisfier factors to the dissatisfiers, as developed by Herzberg.[7] They are far less valuable employees because of this switch. And we should note that people do not make the switch because they want to, but because the rules force them to.

One day we may have the studies and research needed to help each individual set the optimum time for his retirement from a company or agency. We have all seen an individual who should probably have retired at 45, or 50, or 60. We have also seen the individual whose retirement before 70 or 80 would be a great loss. There is, in other words, nothing magic in the age of 65. About all that can be said for it is that it appears to save supervisors and managers the embarrassment of deciding (and of telling an individual) that he and the company must now split. It is also said to make room for younger people. This is an important consideration, but it is an advantage only if the

6. S. D. Saleh: "A Study of Attitude Change in the Pre-retirement Period," in *Journal of Applied Psychology*, 48:310–12 (1964).
7. Herzberg, *op. cit.*

younger people are better qualified. There is no relationship between age and motivation, as Herzberg and a dozen other psychologists have shown in their behavioral studies.

In the meantime, for lack of sound scientific facts, we must do the best we can with what we have. We take 65 or 70 as the end point of a career, and we plan accordingly.

RETIREMENT PLANNING

Anyone who sees people 65 or older as starting their golden years, or who thinks of hobbies and crafts as something older people ought to use to fill up their days, has never really thought carefully about the matter. Many well-intentioned people go around prattling about senior citizens and retirement subdivisions where you put people over 65 to finish out their final days in security and comfort, with perhaps an occasional trip to Bermuda or Hawaii. Here we have the nation's most experienced people set aside as of a certain date to pass their remaining lifetime in leisure worlds. What a waste!

The planning that managers need to think about has two objectives. The first is to help the individual in an organization to make sensible, practical plans about his retirement, *from the beginning of his career.* We do this in the same way we go about insurance planning—and indeed insurance and pensions need to complement each other. This calls for periodic discussion-lectures by experts (for all employees), and for periodic issuance of brochures on the subject, especially as there are changes in Social Security or pension plans.

The second objective is to plan with individuals on ways to capitalize on their experience with the company or agency, *for the benefit of the organization itself,* following their technical retirement. Some of the ways (involving contracts rather than salaries for services rendered) are:

■ Preparing brochures on retirement and what it can mean in terms of further service.

■ Undertaking special studies for the organization in subject-matter areas where more facts are needed. A good idea might be to start with retirement itself. We need facts very badly here, and no one seems to be doing very much about it.

■ Preparing bulletins or brochures on various aspects of the organization's activities.

■ Preparing and publishing summaries or histories of the company, business, or agency, of value in the orientation of new recruits.

■ Undertaking certain public relations activities of use to the organization. Who knows the outfit better than its most experienced people?

■ Preparing and publishing books about the importance of the organization's work.

■ Lecturing both inside and outside the organization on various phases of the work. Inside, we use the material for the training of new people just entering.

■ Helping representatives of other agencies or companies in underdeveloped countries on projects that can help to make the world a better place to live in.

You can think of many other ways to utilize the long experience and developed judgment of an organization's retirees. We might well use the word *alumni* here instead of retirees. Universities get all they can out of their alumni—and not just money, but contributions in real service. Why not, in other words, really make use of the organization's alumni, in the innumerable ways there are to do this? Don't push 'em too hard; after all, they're out of the rat race you're still in, and they may not take kindly to pressure they don't have to put up with any longer! Some of them won't respond. But a great many of these so-called senior citizens have a lot to offer, in their own time, and because they believe in the worth of the organization in which they spent most of their careers.

SOME KEY PROBLEMS IN CAREER SYSTEMS

In the operation of a complete career system several problems may be encountered that are by no means easy to solve:

1. Refusal by Employee to Move

The managing heads, trying always to fill each vacancy with the best qualified person, may discover that their chosen candidate has no intention of leaving the place where he is. He may have bought a home or a small farm, his wife may be teaching in a local school, the family like where they are and have no intention of moving anywhere else, and so on. In other words, for many personal reasons he prefers strongly to stay put. We are assuming here that the promotion means a move, a not uncommon situation in larger organizations.

If he is permitted to refuse the promotion, the organization must then fill the job with its second-best candidate. Also, the career line or ladder is now plugged by the individual who refuses to move. If the person is not permitted to refuse, then he may quit—and thereby the company or agency loses one of its best people. A very neat problem indeed.

The solution that seems to have been the most successful is to develop the *custom* in the organization of moving whenever the need is clear. This takes a series of actions:

■ A written policy is developed setting forth as a requirement that all personnel are expected to accept transfers unless a really serious health problem prevents this, or the employee would suffer serious financial loss.

■ The policy is clearly explained to all new recruits, who may be asked to agree to it in writing.

■ Early training is conducted at a location different from the permanent location. In the first year, then, all new people may move.

■ The policy is systematically carried out in all administrative actions taken, with rare exceptions.

Even this approach has not always worked in organizations that have used it, but it has reduced substantially the number of refusals. In dealing with the really stubborn employee, a manager has to balance his value to the organization against the damage to the career system. Note that if one employee gets away with a refusal to transfer, other employees will perceive that the career policy doesn't really work. "They didn't move Joe— and I don't have to move either."

2. Resentment Against Outsiders Brought In

If promotion is generally from within an existing body of people in the organization, after a while the people will strongly resent bringing in someone from outside. Needed here is a clear statement of policy that sets up the rules of the game. The conditions under which an outsider may be brought in should be specified so that all employees will know what they are.

Such a policy should be thought through with great care, preferably with the full participation of the employees themselves. Few will object to bringing in an individual possessing an expertise simply not available in the organization. But one policy I have encountered in several concerns states essentially that "all other things being equal, the best qualified candidate will be selected." This policy is not always palatable to insiders.

If the company or agency sees that a particular outsider is far and away the best qualified for a position—compared to any contender inside—then it would seem only sensible to recruit the outsider. Such a move ought to make the organization stronger, and thus all the people already in it would benefit. The trouble comes in the sharply divided opinions generated about the outsider versus certain insiders. The managing heads can overrule employee opinion in such a case—provided always that the outsider really *is* better qualified. In doing so, though, they may do damage to their career system. Possibly employee participation in such a case might help to provide a solution.

3. *Unions and Career Systems*

A third problem has to do with the attitude of unions and how they may view the operation of a career system. In the experience of some companies and agencies, unions have interposed no objections to the development of one or several aspects of career development. But this is a highly unsatisfactory state of affairs. If unions are sincerely interested in furthering the welfare of their members, then the top union officials need to do a lot more homework than some of them have done.

Unions, no less than management, should be fostering the best policies and approaches known in providing meaningful work and satisfying careers for people at work. Rather than merely "interposing no objections," union officials should be in there helping to make things better. It is not enough to redress grievances and press for better working conditions. Unions as well as management should be aware of the new and exciting developments in the fields of human behavior, motivation, communications, and employee relations that are coming from the studies of the social scientists. Given this knowledge, unions can help management to do a really sound and constructive job of career development.

I want to be understood at this point as being highly in favor of good unions. I think the working world of this country is far better off now than it would have been had unions never done the job they have. What I am saying is, though, that it is now high time for unions to play a more creative, indeed a nobler, role than they have so far in making the world a better place to work in. Where unions are not changing in this changing world of ours, perhaps managers should undertake to help them.

4. Seniority

A problem almost sure to appear in any career system is the problem of seniority. Great numbers of people still feel most sincerely that promotion should be based on seniority. To promote a younger person "over the heads" of people with twice as much service is bound to cause bitterness in an organization where people think this way.

The fact that an organization succeeds in close proportion to the excellence of its people, plus the fact that good people are good for an organization, is simply not clear to many experienced workers. Usually this is so because in the past things haven't been that way. "This guy got promoted because he knows a guy upstairs—and here I've been for twenty years without getting anywhere." Or "That guy has the superintendent's arm around him, and there's eight or ten guys here—*under him*—who know more than he ever will about the job."

Our past has a way of catching up with us. To construct a really fine career system means in some organizations a pulling out of the morass of previously poor management. This is not easy; it is often incredibly difficult.

There is now little doubt, though, that such long-held opinions and attitudes can be changed.[8] This has been done in a number of organizations. It depends very importantly, indeed critically, on enlisting the help of the employees themselves in effecting the changes; that is, it depends on the full use of participation. Dr. Alfred Marrow's work offers numerous successful examples of what has been done in a large number of successful businesses and industries.

8. See especially *The Failure of Success*, edited and partly written by Alfred J. Marrow (New York: Amacon, 1972).

SUMMARY

What we have done in setting out the elements of a career system is to indicate five general areas of activity:

- Recruitment and selection
- Placement
- Training
- Promotion
- Retirement

Appropriate attention needs to be given to each area of action all the time. The activities are intended to cover the entire careers of people who enter and ultimately leave the organization.

No one can say that the foregoing ideas or principles are gospel, nor can it be said that they will always work. Any reading of the more recent works of Likert, McGregor, Herzberg, McClelland, Ford, Marrow, and numerous other psychologists and sociologists will show that the ideas suggested are generally scientifically sound. They coincide with the opinions and experience of thousands of highly successful supervisors. And they have been in use in a number of industries and government agencies for a period of years long enough to prove their worth.

Most people who have studied the matter generally agree that we need much more certain information and carefully ascertained facts about people and their careers. We need to know a great deal more about how to develop and operate a sound career system. But in the meantime, though, why not try the best we *do* know?

3

Training Systems

TRAINING MEANS MANY THINGS to many people. Academic people tend to deprecate training and are often at pains to distinguish carefully between training and education. They will tell you that they deal in education; whatever training may be needed can come from employers. The amusing thing is, though, that when you train someone you have an objective clearly in mind that you want him to reach, and pity that it is, this isn't true of much of our education.

Basic ideas about training, especially training methods, have already been talked about a good bit. Here, we intend to consider certain ideas or requirements, not so much of training itself, but rather of the parts of a system by means of which effective training can be accomplished in an organization of some size.

Before we begin the delineation of a general training system, though, we need to consider just what training—properly conducted—can do for an organization. There is a good deal of confusion about this. Many managers somehow think of training as a sort of extra activity or perhaps as a reward for a well-done job. Possibly a majority of managers cut the training budget first when times get tough—the very time when training is needed most. Some managers check thoughtfully to keep fully aware of how training is being done, but many don't. Some are content to appraise the value of training by asking a few trainees, "How was the training conference?" If the trainees say they enjoyed it, the conference is deemed to have been a success. This is pure nonsense. The question is not whether they enjoyed it, but whether they learned what they were supposed to.

The whole intent of training should be to qualify people for their work or their jobs, and additionally to qualify them for jobs of greater difficulty and responsibility. Notice there are *two* objectives here—one, training for the job; the other, training for a more important job. Almost everyone agrees on the first objective; after all, it makes sense to have well-trained people on any job. The second objective is not so clear to many managers. Why train people for something they may not do or get to do until sometime in the future? Answering this question is one of the important goals of this chapter. Here, we may simply say that the second objective is relevant only in organizations that have a career system—one that involves the development of men and women for the greater responsibilities and problems of a career ladder.

TRAINING FOR TWO OBJECTIVES

Three types of training are used to accomplish the first objective—to qualify people for their new jobs—as soon as possible:

1. *Orientation training,* aimed at getting a new employee acquainted with the organization and the part he will play in it.

2. *Job training,* aimed at getting the employee into full production on the job as quickly and correctly as possible.

3. *Refresher training,* aimed at keeping people up to date on new methods and ideas pertaining to their jobs.

These kinds of training are not necessarily distinct, but all three must be taken care of, and in about the order shown. Any training system should provide for all of them.

There is left the other objective: to qualify people to perform in jobs that are more important and responsible than the jobs for which they have already been trained. Training in this area has been called *developmental* or *career training*. This kind of training cannot really start until the people involved are fully qualified in the jobs they are already performing. Once qualified, then the training for more responsibility can begin.

Training for supervisory positions obviously falls in this category. So does technical training intended to improve the qualifications of technical specialists (for example, engineers, accountants, scientists, computer specialists). Almost no one ever begins his first job as a supervisor. He is employed because he has other knowledge or skills. Any organization needs good supervisors, and thus every organization should be training its best candidates to become good at supervision. After all, there is some turnover among supervisors.

THE COST AND VALUE OF TRAINING

All training costs money. The problem is: How much can we afford to spend on training? As it happens, there is a very real and clear answer to this question, as applied to any specific job in any organization.

We may take job training of a technical specialist as an example. This is training aimed at getting a new employee into production as soon as possible. We first list all the things new employees must know and be able to do in their jobs. Next, we find out how long it takes, on the average, to learn all such things. This we find out by checking with supervisors experienced in training technical specialists (for example, engineers, accountants, scientists of many kinds, computer specialists).

It may take a new employee an average of, say, a year, to become fully productive. (Note that this average time varies with jobs; it takes longer to train engineers, for instance, than to train file clerks.) People vary also in the rate at which they can learn, but experienced supervisors know very well what the average is.

We will assume here that there has not been any particularly systematic training—that a new person simply learns gradually by observation and by being told what to do. If it takes about a year to get the new person fully producing, then let us note one cost that is quite clear—his annual salary.

We can put this in graph form to see it easily, as in Figure 3. If the new employee's salary is, say, $10,000 per year, then we can begin to fill in the graph, as in Figure 4.

Notice now that in the hypothetical case shown in Figure 4 the employee earns about half his salary the first year. We've paid him $10,000, but in terms of what he produced—*after* he knew how—he gave us only $5,000 worth of production. Notice something else here: the completely untrained employee (at the zero starting point) is the most expensive employee on the payroll. This is because he is paid for practically no production. Not until he is fully trained does he earn the $10,000 a year, that is, *after* the first year.

Now, suppose it were possible, with the help of a well-organized, systematic training program, to get the new employee up to the level of full production in 6 months instead of a year. If we could do this, then our graph might look like Figure 5.

In this graph, the shaded area shows the amount of production we gain by cutting the training time from 1 year to 6 months. Actually, the shaded area is half the old area in which we formerly lost $5,000. We have therefore picked up $2,500 worth of production. Our loss is now cut to $2,500.

Thus, when we ask the question: How much can we afford to spend on training in this case?, the answer is $2,500. If we can do the training for *less* than $2,500, we can make a profit in productivity realized.

If we had, say, 500 people a year to train, then the total we could afford to spend on training should not exceed 500 × $2,500, or $1,250,000. If it exceeds that amount, we're losing money. If it is *less*, then we make a proportionate profit. This is why efficiency of training is important.

Figure 3

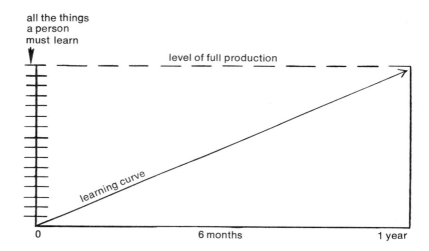

Figure 4

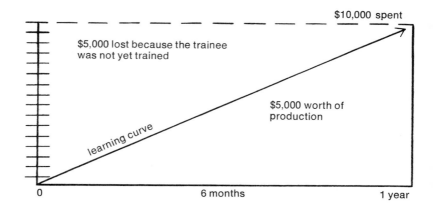

Figure 5

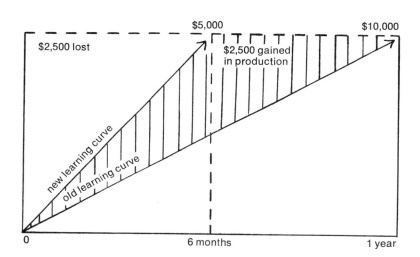

Notice that we do have to spend money to realize this profit. But of course, if we spent no money, we'd lose it anyway.

SUPERVISORY RESPONSIBILITY FOR TRAINING

Training is a supervisory responsibility. Unless this is understood in an organization, the chances for success of training efforts are pretty slim. This responsibility cannot be given away, delegated, or neglected. A training officer, plus a large training staff, cannot possibly conduct the training of every employee in the company or the agency. Nor can a personnel department. It is the supervisor who comes to know his people better than anyone else. He learns their backgrounds and experience, their ambitions, their strong points, their weak points, what they can do well, what they have difficulty doing. He learns such things about his people if he is alert and observant, as a good supervisor must be.

Becoming familiar with the characteristics of his people, the supervisor is in the best position to point to various training needs for each of them. As he appraises and evaluates performance, he learns each person's shortcomings. And, if he is a good supervisor, he will press for training needed to bolster the weak points.

It is obvious, of course, that a supervisor cannot actually do all the teaching or training himself. There may well be many areas of knowledge or of special skills that require a specialist of one sort or another. But it is the supervisor who should make the arrangements or get them started. And his people must always understand that their supervisor is the one responsible.

ELEMENTS OF A TRAINING SYSTEM

We are going to assume here that an organization has a true career system. Where this is really so, a new recruit is offered a job with the company or agency *as a first step* in a career that may very possibly extend for the duration of his working life. People are seldom or never hired by such an organization merely to fill a vacancy. They are employed with the idea that they will be encouraged and helped to go as far in the organization as their abilities and skills will take them.

This calls for a training system that is effective from the time a young man or woman is first recruited, to a period after retirement occurs. The myriad variations in private companies and government agencies—their structure, staffing, size, operations, and objectives—make it impossible to specify *one* training system. Yet, despite this diversity, certain elements enter into most training systems.

1. The New Employee

The training of every new employee should start the day he or she enters on duty. The methods to use must necessarily vary with the kind of organization. An organization that is physically located all in one building could certainly approach its orientation training differently than an organization widely scattered throughout the country or even internationally. The question is not *whether* it should be done, but *how*.

The first important point here is that we simply cannot be content to put the new recruit under his supervisor and "let nature take its course." If the supervisor happens to be a sour apple, our new recruit will become sour also. If the supervisor is a poor teacher, our trainee will be slow to learn—and this is costly. If the supervisor happens not to like the organization, the new recruit can scarcely be expected to become a devoted, loyal employee.

All this leads to a simple idea: The *first* supervisor of a new recruit should be a good one—good teacher, loyal employee, excellent worker, successful supervisor. Such supervisors are not too common. They must be searched out.

Another point: The first day on the job is a day nearly all people remember. First impressions appear to be very important. So, we need to be sure that the first day of a recruit is well handled. Can all supervisors do this? Obviously not. Which ones can, therefore, is important to know. And what recruits learn the first day may well shape their future in the organization.

In sum, therefore, picking the first people to start training recruits may well prove to be of crucial importance. And in a well-managed training system, this must be provided for.

It is also worth noting that job training as well as orientation training can often be done in small groups—which is less expensive than individual, custom training. Choice of the trainer depends largely on his or her ability as a teacher.

Several objectives must be kept in mind with respect to the training of a new employee:

1. To introduce him to the organization and to show him the part he will be expected to play in it. Indeed, this is the objective of orientation training. If a good job is done here, the new employee should be convinced that he has entered an excellent organization in which he can hope to be of real service in the world.

2. To get the new employee into full production in his job just as rapidly as possible.

3. To get the employee interested and active in his own self-development. The third objective is often overlooked. By every possible means, the employee should be encouraged to read, to study, and to think about the kind of work he is performing and the ways in which he can improve his knowledge and skills necessary to perform it.

2. *The Employee After Initial Training*

Once an employee is well oriented and fully into production on his job, his further training can then go forward. Here again are three objectives:

1. To keep him up to date on methods, techniques, and principles applicable to the job he has. This is often called refresher training. It is usually not continuous, since changes don't come all that often, but it should not be neglected.

2. To encourage further study aimed at improving his skill and knowledge about other, more responsible jobs in the organization.

3. To begin his career training. By this time, our career employee should have begun thinking of what he wants to do in the future. A good supervisor can discover by discussion at appropriate times what kind of work his people prefer, their hopes, and their ambitions. Career training can be planned to help them in their chosen directions.

We may note here that an employee one to two years into his job doesn't necessarily understand much about supervision. So we start the training of *all* employees in the basic elements of supervising.

The very things a supervisor needs to learn are, for the most part, things all workers need to learn. For example, supervisors need to learn about human behavior and what motivates people. They need this knowledge in their function of supervision. But then, of course, all workers in an organization need to know something about human behavior, too. After all, everyone has to work with other people. With this idea in mind, training all personnel in the elements of human behavior makes good sense. The people who ultimately become supervisors will make use of such training in their daily work. And the people who never become supervisors can use it too—less often, certainly less intensively—but use it they will.

Thus, training in human relations and behavior ought to start fairly soon after an individual has fully learned his or her job. This is equally important for those people who ultimately become supervisors and those who do not. We could say the same thing about communications and about organizations, especially the one the people are in.

3. The Developing Employee

As time goes on and an employee advances in the organization, each promotion requires the same kind of training used for a new recruit, viz., orientation in the new position, production training in it, refresher training, and continued developmental or career training.

TRAINING DEVICES

The various devices or techniques or methods used for training in an organization will necessarily be different in different companies or agencies. A few devices, however, are worth outlining because, properly adapted, they may have very wide application.

1. Record Keeping

The first of these is the simple matter of records. Some kind of arrangement, preferably simple, needs to be made to keep a record of each individual's training and progress. The obvious place is in the personnel file or folder for each employee. These records, systematically kept, can have much to do with later promotions. They should never be neglected.

2. Home Study Courses

Home study courses, formerly called correspondence courses, have been used with success in many organizations whose offices are far-flung geographically. They can be used to reach even the most remote locations.

Several things seem to be important in using them. One is that the employee ought to be encouraged (but *not required*) to take them. Home study courses are hard work and they take a real determination on the part of any student. The unmotivated student becomes a dropout.

A second matter of importance is to require any employee wishing to take such a course to develop and hand in a plan and schedule he will pursue in taking the course. He should sign this, and so should his supervisor. The employee will usually think twice about dropping out if his boss has okayed the course to begin with.

A third matter deserving attention is the selection of teachers in the organization. Better to use line supervisors or staff people for this, than to use training officers and their assistants. The teachers should be volunteers, and one of the extra benefits here is that the teachers themselves must update their own knowledge of the subject matter in order to keep up with their students.

The preparation of such home study courses can usefully be done by technical experts on the subject matter working with training officers who should be expert on educational methods.

3. Training Centers

Many companies and agencies have developed training centers. Some are quite elaborate installations with large buildings housing training facilities and quarters for the participants. Others are simply locations where facilities and housing may be available in hotels, motels, or other conference facilities.

The intent of a training center, though, is to bring qualified expert teachers to a location to teach selected employees. Courses generally tend to be intensive, both for learning purposes and because long courses cost more than shorter ones.

Selection of employees to go to the center should depend on a clear need for each employee to be there. There is no point in sending an employee to the center just because there is a course and the employee can be spared.

Training center operation is costly. The decision to hold a course there rather than depend on supervisors to do the same job at home, so to speak, ought to be made with a clear understanding of the costs and benefits involved. It may cost more to send a group of people to a training center, but if the experts doing the teaching can offer substantially more than most supervisors can, it makes sense to use the center.

Training officers can be of great help in center operations. They can make all necessary arrangements, develop the courses with the help of staff experts, discover the most expert teachers (both inside and outside the organization) and monitor and help evaluate the courses given.

4. University Work

In some organizations, the need for special training—either administrative or technical—may best be met by sending employees to a university. The courses may be short, or they may run a full year, depending on need. In either case, the training officer should spend some time at several universities discussing his organization's needs and the university's offerings.

Many universities are now tailoring courses to fit company or agency needs. Many others simply offer a sort of cafeteria of ongoing courses at the university. Which is the wiser choice needs to be carefully considered.

Obviously, this device is possibly the most expensive of all, since it is costly to send a person or persons to a university, especially for one or two semesters. Some organizations use this device as a sort of final polishing of the training of its most promising career people. These are the people about to assume really key positions in the organization.

5. Individual Work

In addition to the more formal, organized types of training, supervisors need to be alert for training opportunities suitable to one or another of their people. These opportunities may include work on special task forces or committees; loans to other organizations for special work; visits to research institutions, experiment stations, and similar institutions; visits to or assignments to other segments of the organization, and so on. In every case the supervisor will do well to require a written report, possibly to have the employee present an oral report to the rest of the unit, and certainly to make a record of the assignment for inclusion in the personnel file.

6. Supplementary Reading

Not all knowledge comes from books, but a great deal of it can and does. Serious career employees need to know what's going on in the world that may affect their jobs or their organization. They can get a good deal of this by reading and study on their own.

It is a wise organization that requires its top staff people to keep a flow of useful and important information reaching all employees or important groups of them. Liberal policies on purchasing books, brochures, article separates, and the like, help to keep the information flowing. The information should be of help to supervisors, managers, technical experts, and the employees generally. Discussing such publications in supervisors' staff meeting helps materially to keep people aware of and alive to new ideas.

7. *Retirement Training*

Although one can scarcely specify subject matter for training in general, the subject of retirement comes pretty close to being a must somewhere in every training program.

From the beginning of his career, an employee should learn and understand about retirement and the policies and mechanisms in use in the company or agency. How his insurance policies may coincide with pension payments, how to avoid overinsurance, whether to contribute extra funds to the retirement fund, income taxes, etc., need to be explained and discussed in full. As time goes on, pension or retirement plans change, and such changes deserve attention—with *all* employees.

There is really a great deal more to retirement planning than most people think—even some of the people about to retire! Available everywhere are experts from the Social Security Administration, reputable insurance companies, and government agencies. These experts can and should be used from time to time to explain all the "angles" of retirement and its planning. Somewhere, too, in every organization there should be one or more staff officials completely familiar with the retirement plan of the company or agency, Social Security, life insurance, and pension plans of other organizations. Such an expert should know in full detail about these matters so that advice and consultation with employees is correct and practical.

PUTTING IT ALL TOGETHER

From the foregoing discussion, it should be clear that a training system must be continuous if it is to be successful. This does not mean that an employee must be sitting in a training session all his days. But the system should provide for training of people as the needs for training become clear to supervisors and their people.

Once the system is put in outline form, it is wise to place a copy in the hands of every supervisor so that there may be no uncertainty about the availability of training. The program needs to extend to every level and to make use of the best educational techniques known.

As time goes on, the training officers should be required to undertake studies to ascertain the effectiveness of the training rendered in relation to its costs. Evaluation of training is not always easy. But no manager would dream of turning out a product without deciding in advance what its specifications must be. Nor should he deal any differently with training.

4

Developing the Supervisor

It is generally recognized that a key element in the effectiveness of any organization is the quality and effectiveness of its supervisors. This being so, it follows that organizations must search out potential supervisors and train them in the knowledge and skills they need to develop to be successful. The recruitment and training of supervisors cannot be ignored or left to chance. Unless these activities are carried on systematically, the chances of developing a highly effective supervisory force are not particularly good. The development of supervisors and managers must be planned for; adequate funds must be devoted to it; intelligent effort must be used to achieve it. All that we know about education and training tells us that this is necessary and wise.

We need to recall that we seldom employ supervisors as such. We take people into our organizations who possess knowledge, skills, or abilities in some field other than that of supervision and management. This means that ultimately managers must select their supervisors from among people trained in something else. It is largely after employees have "learned the business," as we say, that we begin to consider which among them seem to have the makings of good supervisors. It is true that during pre-employment checks and interviews we may note certain qualities in a man or woman that might make him or her a likely candidate for supervisory work. But if we are trying to employ, say, an accountant or an engineer, we usually—and quite correctly—check most closely to be sure that our applicant is first of all a good accountant or a qualified engineer.

This approach to the employment of people leads to the problem of finding supervisors among workers, and of giving them the training necessary to qualify them for this important work. Parenthetically we may note that there is a real advantage in doing this. Any supervisor is expected to be familiar with the kind of work being performed by the people he must supervise. Various studies have shown clearly that supervisors not familiar with the work tend to be rejected by their people. A supervisor has to practice in a certain setting, and if he does not understand that setting, he cannot practice with full effectiveness. He and his people must work together toward goals they all realize and understand, communicating with each other on terms well recognized among them. Here is at least one clearcut advantage in "coming up through the ranks."

INDICATORS OF SUPERVISORY POTENTIAL

As we go about making our selection of supervisors, we must learn to recognize a number of indicators of inherent qualities or abilities that can be successfully developed. Some of these are:

1. The person should be doing a good job in the work for which he was originally hired. This is usually considered an important requisite. Before anyone can be considered for another job—supervisory or any other—it seems only reasonable to expect that he make a success of the job he currently holds. We reason that someone successful in one kind of work may be more likely

to prove successful in another. Of course this is only a sort of working hypothesis. It seems obvious that intelligence can display itself in many ways, but it does not necessarily follow that the best accountant or the best engineer will automatically turn out to be the best supervisor. Unfortunately, experience indicates that the reverse may often be true.

2. In doing the work for which they were originally employed, people may display a number of qualities that we value in supervisors. We may note, for example, that they display enthusiasm, that they possess initiative, and that they are imaginative. We can see that they have the qualities of patience and good humor, and that they are emotionally mature. They may demonstrate good judgment and common sense.

We can observe qualities such as these—and there may very well be others you can think of—in a man or woman who is not performing supervisory work at all. What we are doing here, though, is looking for qualities we would like to see in a supervisor. We are not necessarily looking only for evidences of success in the work the person is performing, because that work is something other than supervision.

3. Closely associated with qualities such as these is an attitude that we should be glad to observe. This is the scientific attitude, a way of thinking about things that leads a person to base conclusions on facts rather than fancy. It is the attitude that causes him continually to ask that all-important question: *why?* Among supervisors of people, we desperately need people who never cease asking that question. It is possibly the tool with the keenest cutting edge of any a supervisor and manager has. It is often considered a great nuisance to have someone barging about an organization asking *why* about everything he does not understand. But of all approaches to a problem, this is possibly the most productive of all. If more supervisors questioned procedures and tried also to discover why people act as they do, just possibly we might be further forward in our dealings with each other.

4. It is well to find out whether a candidate can convey ideas

clearly and well, both as he talks and as he writes. He needs also to demonstrate that he can listen and that he can read. The two major methods we use to communicate—the talking–listening process and the writing–reading process—are methods that must be well developed in supervisors. Certainly, long before anyone becomes a supervisor, and in any of a variety of jobs, we can judge how well he can communicate. We may also be able to discern whether he is likely to be trainable in this important field.

5. Next, an important indicator we may look for is breadth of interest. Specifically, we may note that a person displays an interest in the work of the organization as a whole or of an important segment of it—over and above his own particular job. He may make suggestions for improving the organization, for sharpening its objectives, for greater efficiency of operation, for better coordination, better communications. These suggestions may reveal that he has done some thinking about more than his own particular job. We cannot, of course, recognize this thinking as really substantial unless the proposals are constructive, practical, and clearly unselfish. What we are seeking to learn is whether our candidate has a greater interest than his job, and possibly also the direction in which that interest lies.

6. Lastly, our potential supervisor seems to "get along" well with his associates, his supervisor, and with other people generally. We may assume provisionally that he therefore likes to work with other people, in fact, may have a decided preference in this direction. Further than simply "getting along" with other people, some individuals may turn out to be among those whose opinions are sought and respected by their associates. Consciously or unconsciously they are gradually becoming leaders of informal groups of employees. These informal groups are usually well known to the perceptive supervisor, as are their leaders.

Now it cannot be argued that unless every one of the indicators mentioned above is displayed, we do not have a potential supervisor. I doubt that all supervisors—good ones, too—are fully and perfectly equipped with such a laundry list of qualities, attitudes, and abilities. Nevertheless, we need to search for such characteristics thoughtfully and skillfully. Many of them are easy to overlook. Worse, some of them may be obscured or overshadowed by characteristics that may be excellent in the job the person is in, but that are not really what is needed in a supervisor and manager.

The business of searching out supervisory characteristics among nonsupervisory people is an important job that falls to the experienced and capable supervisor to perform. The best supervisors we have are those who are clearly recognized as developers of people. The recognition of supervisors for good work in uncovering potential supervisory talent, and for developing the people who display it, is a matter of importance in an organization. If the administrative climate of an organization is conducive to this, we may justifiably hope to discover most of the considerable supervisory talent that may exist.

Once an individual is noted who seems to have the right kind of qualities, the next tentative step is to begin testing him. We check by giving him simple assignments at first, to see how he responds. If he does well with a little more responsibility, a somewhat greater challenge, then we give him something more. Assuming he responds, we reach the point after a time where we need to talk with him seriously about his interests and ambitions. This is an important step—a crucial one. If he is really interested enough to want to make a career of supervision, then we may begin his supervisory training in earnest. If he prefers to remain in his technical or substantive field, then we ordinarily do not undertake to make him into a supervisor willy-nilly. It is unwise to "push" anyone into this work. A person should go into it only because he wants to and with his eyes wide open.

For example, suppose we have a group of engineers. Among them are two individuals who exhibit supervisory abilities. On checking, we find that one is wedded to engineering, lives it, loves it, wants an *engineering* career, and nothing else. The other has become interested in the workings of the organization, the ways in which people are dealt with, or some other administrative issues. He exhibits real interest in these phases of the work and is willing to subordinate his engineering to do work that requires not engineering but management skills.

This choice, between administrative and technical work, is a hard one to make. A person whose formal training has been entirely technical should be led to see that, while this training will continue to be useful to him, it must be supplemented and to an increasing extent give way to another kind of training—that is, in management work. It must be made very clear to him that he stands at a crossroads, that he may go a little way down the management road and still be able to turn back, but that the farther he goes the harder it will be to reverse himself. He may try the management road for a period—perhaps for a year or two—and still be able to recover, say, as a professional engineer. He has a trial period, so to speak, in which he can come to know his own mind, and during which supervisors will evaluate his supervisory development. Finally there will come a time when he must stand forth and be counted—engineer? Or supervisor?

WHAT SUPERVISORS MUST BE ABLE TO DO

Successful supervisors are usually found to be highly skilled in doing a number of things. A list of these follows, but it should be pointed out first that exactly *how* supervisors do these things is what really counts; that is the art of supervision. It is much like the art of a pianist. A would-be pianist can be taught how to read music, how to play scales, how to use the piano pedals, how chords are put together, what harmony means, and so on. But in the end we have to say to him—now, *you* try to make good music! So, with a supervisor, we can show him and teach him such skills as he must have, but in the end we must say—now go ahead and supervise the very best way you can.

With this preliminary then, able supervisors are skilled in doing the following:

1. Gain the willing and interested participation of their people in doing work, and in attaining the objectives of their organization. With experience, they become skilled in learning and understanding why each of their people acts as he does.

2. Communicate well, that is, they know how to listen, they know how to talk, they know how to write, and they know how to read. There are techniques for doing each of these; one does not necessarily learn them in school.

3. Train and develop people, not only for the jobs at hand, but also for jobs involving greater responsibilities.

4. Look ahead and consider what they want their organization to be doing at certain future times; that is, they know how to plan, and to schedule.

5. Analyze workloads, and thereby avoid either overloading or overstaffing, and assign kinds of work appropriate to the qualifications of their various people.

6. Make decisions, in a timely way, and on the basis of both the facts they can get and the imponderables they must often weigh for lack of enough facts.

7. Judge the quality of work, and they are aware of the need for technical standards against which they can measure work.

8. Organize people, ideas, and materials so that there is little or no waste effort involved in getting the work done.

9. Improve operating efficiency, and they work with their people in employing this knowledge in a systematic way.

Potential supervisors can be trained in all these skills. There are well-known, well-tested techniques for doing them that are widely available in many books. Many men and women are excellent teachers in one or another of these skills. Thus, the problem of training potential supervisors may not be as difficult as it may appear at first sight. Given a specific listing of skills and kinds of knowledge a person must have to perform supervisory work with excellence, it is obvious that an organization should be able to marshal its forces so as to train its potential supervisors in the art. What it takes is good planning and careful scheduling, preceded of course by the realization that such training is of key importance to the success of the organization.

Many opportunities for training supervisors exist. A number of universities are now offering courses in various phases of management. It is possible for a supervisor almost anywhere to take advantage of short courses, special courses, workshops, institutes, home study courses, and so on. Even so, any agency or organization is wise to recognize that a single course of study is not all that is necessary for the development and training of supervisors. No one becomes a successful supervisor after a few days or a few weeks of instruction. It takes much more than that. In college terms, it takes really a whole curriculum, not just a single course. Such courses can have greatest value when they are considered as part of a comprehensive training plan devised by an agency or company for the development of its supervisory force. When they are considered in this light, rather than as a one-shot panacea, courses of this kind are indeed much needed and highly useful.

FOUR FACTORS FOR SUPERVISORY SUCCESS

There are four factors on which supervisory success seems to depend (we have already considered two of them):

- The ability and skill of the supervisor
- The willingness of the supervisor
- The authority of the supervisor to act
- The administrative courage of the supervisor

Each of these factors is important, and no one of them can be effective unless the others are also operative. They are much like the classic example of the chair: no single leg can support the seat; two legs cannot do it; nor can three legs very satisfactorily; all four legs are necessary if the seat is to remain standing and secure. Thus, a willing supervisor armed with necessary authority may do a great deal of damage if he lacks the ability to supervise people effectively, or the confidence he needs to act. A skillful, willing, and courageous supervisor cannot be effective without authority to act. Nor is it likely that much will be accomplished by an able supervisor who is unwilling to act, even though he has the requisite authority. Given all four factors in full operation, however, the plans of the organization can be carried out and the objectives reached, once the supervisors are set in action.

We have already discussed briefly some ideas about the basic training of supervisors. Given good basic training then, a supervisor begins to develop as his carefully evaluated experience enriches his understanding. We can expect this development, and we need to guide it and encourage it. In doing this we strengthen one of the four legs of our theoretical chair.

With respect to willingness, we should recall the ideas already considered about recruiting supervisors. If we find our supervisor unwilling, it just could be that he took the job because he was urged into it. He may have been oversold in the first place. Worse, he may have taken on the work because it paid better or to enjoy the added status. There may, in fact, be many reasons why he took the job, none or only some of which were the right ones. Later on, our supervisor may discover that all is not as rosy as he thought it was going to be. He gets into seriously complex problems that are extremely difficult to solve. Some of his decisions may backfire. He becomes hesitant. He begins to dread the days. He becomes unwilling. And the work goes to pot.

For such simple reasons, any new supervisor must be closely observed throughout his first months, even his first couple of years. All is not lost if he does not come up to expectations. Remember, we converted a good man in the first place. Our (and his) judgment could have been wrong. If this becomes clear, *then* is the time to correct the error, giving him every possible means of saving face. Some organizations neglect this trial period; they keep hoping for the best for ten or fifteen years or longer. But then it is far too late.

Managers need supervisors with confidence in themselves, with a high degree of interest in people, and with enthusiasm for supervisory work. When we have men and women like this, we have a willingness to try, a willingness to act. And willingness we must have if our supervisory development is to succeed.

Next, we may consider a third factor affecting the success of supervisors, their authority. This is a matter that is so confused in many organizations as to require some attention.

Both in government and industry many questions have been raised about the status and authority of the supervisor. These questions apply primarily to foremen in industry and to first-line supervisors in the government, although the questions affect nearly all supervisory personnel except possibly those classed as "top management." The principal questions are:

- What authority does a supervisor need, how much does he have, and is what he has sufficient?

- Are supervisors actually part of the "rank and file," or are they part of management, or are they somewhere in between?

Richard S. Halpern has discussed these questions from the point of view of industrial foremen.[1] He found that many foremen maintained they were bypassed by management in various ways, that they were not fully informed about what management was doing or intended to do, and that unions were regularly undercutting their authority. This was a far cry from the days when foremen reigned supreme in their units. In earlier times they could hire, fire, discipline, set wages, and settle grievances. Very steadily, however, these authorities have been eroded. Some

1. "Employee Unionization and Foreman's Attitudes," in *Administrative Science Quarterly*, 6:73–88 (1961).

have been reserved to people higher up in the company; some have been modified or nullified by union contracts. It is, therefore, not surprising to find that some foremen are uncertain of themselves, and that they are asking where they stand.

Similar questions are often asked by government supervisors. They never could hire, fire, discipline, set wages, or settle grievances altogether independently. This authority in the government has generally been reserved either to heads of agencies, to the Civil Service Commission, or to the Congress. On the other hand, it seems true that some of the authority supervisors need has been modified or nullified by personnel staff units. As examples, training is often lifted bodily out of the hands of supervisors and performed by training staffs: awards (for example, bonuses for good work) are handled by committees rather than by supervisors; in some agencies the supervisor is permitted to play little if any part in the recruitment and selection of people for his unit, and in some agencies, personnel problems are either lifted out of the hands of supervisors, or he hands them over to personnel staffs in the belief that he has no responsibility for dealing with such problems. You may feel that this sort of thing does not happen in your organization, or you may recognize that some such things do. They are not universally true, but they do occur.

It is generally customary, in considering what authority a supervisor has, to discuss whether he can hire, fire, discipline, set pay rates, settle grievances, and the like. But our supervisor— any supervisor anywhere—has another kind of authority within himself, as a person, to get things done. For example:

- He can listen carefully to what his people tell him, and try to understand their meaning and their point of view.
- He can try to be clear in talking to his people, avoiding the semblance of authoritarian power.
- He can gain the confidence of his people by supporting them as needed.
- He can get his people to work *with* him instead of *for* him, more especially as he displays his own confidence in them.

■ He can be alert and quick to recognize good work his people do, individually and together.

■ He can be constructive in helping his people overcome their errors, and in displaying tolerance toward their mistakes.

■ He can help his people develop their feeling of responsibility, by letting them perform, that is, do their work without excessively close supervision.

■ He can try to recognize changes he may need to make in himself, in order to be more considerate of and more effective with his people.

The interesting thing about such items as the above is that any supervisor can use them as freely as he wishes. This is a completely free area of operation. No rule prevents the use of authority such as this, and there is no procedural red tape in which to become entangled.

I am aware that many supervisors will react against these ideas very strongly. Many old-timers will snort that this sort of stuff is no way to get things done. Isn't it? Prof. Herbert A. Simon[2] of Carnegie Tech remarked some years ago: "Man does not generally work well with his fellowman in relations saturated with authority and dependence, with control and subordination, even though these have been the predominant relations in the past. He works much better when he is teamed with his fellowman in coping with an objective, understandable, external environment." Research having to do with people as they work in organizations lends conclusive support to this idea. Very possibly this way of thinking, this attitude toward people, may come to be the predominant idea in the relations between supervisors and the people with whom they work. It may be that our traditional ideas about the authority that supervisors have or don't have may be found, after thorough study, to be of much less consequence than we think.

And now, for the fourth leg of the chair—a supervisor's ad-

2. *The New Science of Management Decision*, by Herbert A. Simon. New York: Harper & Row, Publishers, 1960; p. 49.

ministrative courage. By this phrase I mean that quality—needed every day by every supervisor—that enables him to make clear-cut decisions and then to stand firm in carrying them forward. It is this same quality that enables a supervisor to stand up for his people, to defend them, and to protect them. It is a quality that makes it possible for a supervisor to be described as a person who always knows what he is doing and where he is going. We have no doubt as to where he stands. We know he will consider all aspects of a problem before he decides—but when he decides, we know he'll make his decision stick.

A supervisor with administrative courage will never retreat from a difficult problem in the hope that it may go away. He will not display inconsistency in decisions nor falter in pursuing his objective. He will display deep sympathy and kindness in his dealings with people, but he will not let soft sentimentality get in the way of good judgment.

Experienced supervisors will recognize what I am trying to describe. Administrative courage is something one has to develop. This may, on occasion, cause anguish in a supervisor who must take action when it would be easier not to, or who must make a decision contrary to his own personal preferences. The supervisor who lacks administrative courage will not enjoy his work, is not likely to be particularly successful, and indeed, is well advised to try some other, less demanding kind of work.

WHAT MANAGERS EXPECT FROM SUPERVISORS

We come finally to the proof of the pudding. Given adequate selection, good training, careful guidance, what then may we expect from our supervisors?

In general, we can say that managers expect supervisors to be successful in guiding and directing the efforts of a group of people working at specified tasks. When we say this, about all we are saying is that we expect supervisors to do a successful job of supervising—and this is not a very helpful statement in itself. The question really is: What *is* successful? How do we judge supervisory *success?*

There are many ways we can do this, depending on the kind of situation in which a supervisor operates. But in general, in any situation, we must judge a supervisor by *what his people do.* We may consider our supervisor to be no more than an average sort of guy. Or we may decide that he has a great deal of patience, a good sense of humor, is very decisive, and displays considerable initiative. We may observe that he seems to be doing all the things a good supervisor should be doing. But all this is judging the supervisor, not his results. What he achieves must be sought in what his people do, in how well they perform. *These are the results.* We can detect them by watching for such items as these:

■ His people produce whatever it is they are supposed to produce, in goodly quantity and quality. We can tell this from production records and quality checks, as well as from observation. This item is of primary importance; after all, the group of people is set up in the first place to do a job.

■ His people display skill and intelligence in doing their work. We learn this by observing and comparing their efforts with those of others doing similar work or of beginners.

■ His people have confidence in him and willingly follow his lead. We can tell this is so when we see them display loyalty to him or seek his advice on personal as well as official problems. We also can observe them when they try to perform ably, obviously hoping for or expecting his praise.

■ His people seem to enjoy their work. We learn this as we watch their display of interest and zeal in going about their tasks. We may also note it in the low turnover rates.

■ His people develop in stature. By this we mean that they "grow" in their jobs, develop their ability to do more and better work, display imagination in attacking problems, and expand their intellectual attainments. We can also see that other agencies or companies are constantly recruiting people trained under able supervisors. This may be called piracy by some; to me it is evidence of topnotch supervision, and successful supervisors are gratified to see it take place.

In summary, then, we have noted these points:

1. High-quality supervision is essential to the operation of successful organizations.

2. Potential supervisors must be selected from among non-supervisory workers trained in nonsupervisory work. The selection should depend primarily on detection of supervisory qualities, rather than on success in nonsupervisory work.

3. Training of supervisors should be planned on the basis of work supervisors must perform. This training cannot be done on a one-shot basis; it must be done on a curriculum basis, that is, a continuous effort extending over time, carefully planned in advance.

4. Supervisors must be well trained in the knowledge and skills they need for their kind of work. Further, they must be willing, they need the right kind of authority to act, and they had better be well supplied with administrative courage.

5. And finally, supervisors should be judged by what their people do.

5

Span of Control

ONE OF THE BASIC PRINCIPLES of organization is that *the number of people reporting to one supervisor should be no more than the number whose efforts he can effectively direct and coordinate.*[1] This is often called the principle of the span of control. It has caused a great deal of argument among experts. Indeed, how many people can one person supervise? The answer to this question has many important ramifications.

If the span is too narrow, that is, if a supervisor is working with too few people, then he is likely to overdo his supervision. In an effort to keep fully occupied he may be continually breathing down the necks of his people, which is certainly not the way to develop responsibility. In many cases, his people may resent what they may justifiably come to perceive as too close supervision.

Too narrow a span will also obviously result in higher costs than necessary. For example, if we need ten supervisors but have twenty, the costs of supervision are twice what they need

1. See *The Successful Supervisor*, by William R. Van Dersal. New York: Harper & Row, Publishers, 1974. 3d edition, pp. 140–42.

be. And since supervisors are generally paid more than those they supervise, excessive numbers of supervisors will be a relatively high budget item.

If the span is too wide, that is, if a supervisor is trying to work with too many people, he may get hopelessly bogged down. He may lose track of what's going on; he may not be able to devote adequate attention to each and all of his people; and, he may have to spend so much time with them that his other functions may suffer.

The costs of too wide a span are not as easy to see, but they are quite high. They result from frustration of employees who cannot get the advice and counsel they need when they need it. Some of the supervisor's people may assume too much uncontrolled responsibility and ultimately cause difficulties. One or another of his people may even attempt to do a little supervising himself. All sorts of unwanted effects take place, all costing money in wasted effort and overlapping and duplication of functions. Also, we must add the cost of the supervisor's failure to perform his other functions, especially those of planning and organizing work.

Despite some very interesting treatments of this matter of span of control,[2] the plain fact is that it cannot be stated in general, but must be stated in reference to a specific situation. Many textbooks state very positively that 3 to 5 people is the proper span. Most of these base their material on the work of Lyndall Urwick of England. Others (for example, W. W. Suojanen[3]) have "exploded" Urwick's theory and pointed out that there are plenty of successful organizations in which the range is from 1 to 24.

Nevertheless, careful study of spans of control in specific situations has shown that the wisest course is to set up a span

2. See "The Manager's Span of Control," by Lyndall F. Urwick, in *Harvard Business Review* for May–June, 1956.
3. "The Span of Control—Fact or Fable," by W. W. Suojanen in *Advanced Management*, November 1955.

judged to be about right, then to check at intervals to find out whether the judgment was correct. An example of this can be taken from the experience of a government organization dealing in services to farmers.

Area managers in this organization were put in charge of 5 or 6 field offices. This was based on textbook theory of the 3–5 span (slightly stretched because of cost). Within a year it became clear that there were far too many managers. They were literally getting in the way of their field supervisors. So, as opportunity offered, the span was widened. In the next few years, the span was widened first to about 8, then 10, then 12. These are average figures, of course; some supervisors had a few less, some had a few more. The point is, though, that this span of control required continuing attention.

As the span was carefully widened, a few of the managers were purposely given several more field offices than the average. At the end of about 10 years, the average was 12 per manager, but there were a few that were given 14, 16, even 18. By the time it became clear that 12 could readily be handled, some officials wanted to go way on up—to 20 or 25. This, however, was jumping to an unwarranted conclusion, since careful study showed that 13 was about the most that could be expected of most managers *in the existing program.*

At about this same time, the agency was given several new functions to perform, that is, the program was changed from what it was to a larger and broader one. As this took place it became clear that 13 would simply not do. New training efforts had to be made; many adjustments in staff had to be made also. The area managers could no longer handle 13 or more field offices. The number had to be reduced, and was, gradually, after study.

In this example a number of ideas are worth noting:

■ Judgment as to proper size of span of control will vary depending on the organization's objectives, program, functions, and staffing.

- Spans of control require constant monitoring to be sure they are neither too narrow nor too wide.

- Spans of control may need to change as the organization changes its program or operations.

- A span of control found to be well suited to one segment of an organization cannot necessarily be transplanted to other, different segments of the same organization, or to a different organization altogether.

- In evaluating spans of control, a useful device is to give a few managers more, and a few managers less, than the average. These might be thought of as indicators—of whether the average is too high or too low.

Several exceptions to these ideas are fairly obvious. If you have only one manager instead of a number, there will be no such thing as an "average." Other means must be found to decide whether a given span is too wide or too narrow. Some managers are better able than others to organize their work and manage their operations. Individual differences cannot be ignored, but this is not to imply that it pays to keep changing managers.

All the foregoing depends on the assumption that managers as well as supervisors have been well trained. It also assumes that an organization intent on excellence is constantly on the alert not only to improve management but to reduce its costs. As a result, for example, of the above change in span of control from an average of 6 to an average of 12, the total number of area managers was reduced from 350 to fewer than 250. (The numbers were not cut in two because of other factors not germane here.) The average cost per area manager and his office was about $25,000. Total "savings" were therefore about $2,500,000, diverted to other necessary functions.

We should also note that other important factors undoubtedly influence the span of control. One is geographic spread, that is, where people reporting to one supervisor are located at fairly long or very great distances from him. Another is the amount of work other than supervision that a supervisor is expected to perform. The more of this work there is, the less time the supervisor can spend supervising, that is, the narrower his span of control must be. Still another factor is the degree to which policies and procedures are delineated. If policies are largely unwritten and procedures likewise, there will be need for more frequent conferring between supervisors and their people. This means a narrower span of control may be needed. If policies and procedures are clear, written, and well known, less frequent contact may be sufficient, and wider spans might be adequate.

As may be seen, spans of control may vary widely, depending on a number of factors operating individually or in concert. Successful organizations could be cited where a span of control may reach as many as 60 people. This does not mean, however, that they are successful *because* of such a span. It does not mean either that this number is therefore safe in another organization.

The real question about any span of control is: How does it work? Careful monitoring and evaluation must proceed on a continuing basis in order to answer this question. Spans of control are influenced by change, as are any other methods or approaches. Managers will do well to recognize this fact.

6

Performance Appraisals and Goal Setting

A GREAT DEAL has been written about performance appraisals. In general, supervisors are urged to appraise the performance of their people annually, discussing the strengths and weaknesses of each person in an appraisal interview. Usually there is a form of some kind that states what the standards of performance are, with room for plus marks, minus marks, or grades (as 1, 2, 3, etc.). Recent years have seen quite an upsurge in this sort of evaluation procedure.

Employees are said to welcome such appraisals. At long last, it is believed, the employee finds out where he stands and what is expected of him. The employee, it is thought, is very much in favor of the interview.

The fact is that most employees and supervisors alike hate such appraisals. The interviews create uncomfortable situations. They commonly make the employee feel quite unhappy. Many supervisors, for example, feel they must do something to improve employee performance, and they dutifully search for mistakes or poor work that they can urge the employee to correct. On the other hand, some supervisors gloss over actual performance, rate the employee as satisfactory, then go about the business of getting the man fired.

Most of the time, performance appraisals are used as the primary basis for raises or promotions, and where this is so, the discussions between the supervisor and his employee are not really about performance at all, but about whether the employee gets the raise or the promotion. All sorts of unsatisfactory results have come about, both because the *annual* performance appraisal is too late, and because the approach is seldom used with the skill that it requires.

Suggested below is an approach using goal setting that has proven very useful. It is based on experience both in government and industry.[1] It is easy for good supervisors to use and for good managers to set the stage in which it can operate. It is not complex, and it should be kept simple—which is the reason why this chapter is kept relatively brief.

THE SETTING OF GOALS

The first thing we need to know (or to establish) is the major goal or goals of the organization as a whole. These may be quite

1. The reader will have noted that this brief outline is a simple application of "management by objectives," or MBO as the current fad has it. Actually the setting of objectives and appraising performance based on them have been used for a very long time in a great many organizations. Peter Drucker is given credit for the phrase "management by objectives" in his *Practice of Management*, published by Harper & Row in 1954. The reader will also do well to have a look at George S. Odiorne's three books: *Management by Objectives* (New York: Pitman, 1965); *Management Decisions by Objectives* (Englewood Cliffs, N. J.: Prentice-Hall, 1969); and, especially, *Management and the Activity Trap* (New York: Harper & Row, 1974).

"Management by objectives" is a good phrase that expresses a good idea. But like so many other ideas, it has been heavily overemphasized by devoted followers in this country. There is nothing magic in MBO; it is simply one of many good tools that produce good results when they are skillfully used.

broad in scope, but they should define clearly what the organization hopes to do and the basic direction in which it will be heading.

The identification of these goals depends importantly on the managers and executives in the so-called upper echelons of the agency or company, who should get them into writing and see that they are widely disseminated so that all employees may know what they are. They should also be made known to the public. And, as they are changed, the changes should again be widely disseminated.

The second thing we need to do is to establish goals for the various segments or units of the organization. These unit goals should necessarily be consistent with and support the total goals mentioned above. However they will not, of course, be as broad in scope as the total goals.

The third thing we need to establish is goals for the individual worker. These are quite specific as to the kinds of work the employees will perform. And they too must be in full accord with the unit and organization goals.

The setting of goals needs to be done in the order suggested. Individual employee goals can scarcely be set if the unit goals are uncertain or unknown. And unit goals cannot be established if the company or agency doesn't know where it's going.

In establishing goals it is of major importance that the employees participate fully. If the "overall" goal is not something the employee really believes in, he is quite unlikely to work very hard to reach it. In fact, it may be that he is in the wrong organization altogether. If the individual's goal is set *for* him by somebody else, he may not really agree with it, and again, he will probably not try very hard to reach it. What we are after, in other words, is goals that both the employees and the organization believe in and will seek to reach. We want the individuals to want to work toward goals they have a part in setting.

CHARACTERISTICS OF GOALS

■ For the organization. These should show clearly the "bigger meaning" in the program of work. People want to feel that what they are doing is important in the world, that they are performing a service of which they can be proud.

For example, you might set the goal of a garbage-collecting agency as picking up the garbage in 100,000 garbage cans per week and disposing of it. (The employees are expected to cover a certain number of garbage cans per man and dump the contents into trucks. The trucks are to convey the garbage to an incinerator, where it is burned.) That, in the opinion of many people, is all there is to it.

Within this framework, the job of the garbage man is simply a dirty, smelly, unpleasant one. He has (he feels) no status whatever; he is at the bottom of the heap. He just dumps garbage. Not much possibility here for pride in a job well done. And because of this definition of the job, the work is often sloppy and the turnover of employees is high.

But in a larger context, the goal of the agency can—and should—be restated: to help keep the city a healthful, beautiful, and pleasant place in which to live and work, and raise children. In this broader framework, the job of the sanitary technician or sanitation worker[2] is to help bring this situation about. He performs a valuable and important job in doing this work. He can take pride in his work—and so should the people in his city. Furthermore, with this goal in mind, the sanitary technician can take pride in cleaning up the tin cans and paper scraps that often might have been left strewn on the street by the garbage man. He will be more likely to avoid smashing flower beds by throwing can covers into them. He may advise the homeowner about needs for newer, better containers, better placement of them, spraying

2. *Not* garbage man; a title ought to have at least some dignity.

with insecticides and odor-reducing chemicals in hot weather, and so on. The job is as dirty and ill-smelling as ever, but the way the sanitary technician sees it is quite different.

■ For the individual. These goals must show clearly where the individual should be when he finally reaches them—for example, complete twenty-five gizmos by the end of the year, each one of a given description and specified quality. This kind of a goal sets forth both quantity and quality, characteristics which many goals often lack.

Oftentimes these goals can be set (by agreement with the individual, remember) in what amounts to a contract to perform, on a seasonal, quarterly, monthly, weekly, or even daily basis, depending on the kind of work.

In developing these "performance contracts," we need to discuss with each individual what is reasonable to expect. They have been called by the Raytheon management "reasonable expectancies," or REs, a very useful term and concept. What this is for any given goal can be found in the answer to the question: What can the average worker (not the top performer!) do, per year, per month, per week, etc., in this particular job? Given the answer (which is found from experience in the past and/or in comparison to closely similar jobs), we can then say to the individual: "It seems reasonable to expect that you can do X amount of work of specified quality per year, month, week, or whatever. Other workers have done it; you can do it too. Are you willing to try?"

The goal or goals should be set down in writing. If they're oral only, there is too much chance that there may be disagreement about them later on. The supervisor may remember them one way, the employee may remember them differently. Discussed fully, and put in written form, there is much less likelihood of misunderstanding. The supervisor should always seek to find out whether his employee does fully understand what is written down. Words often mean one thing to one person and quite another to someone else.

APPRAISAL OF PERFORMANCE

Once the individual's goals have been established—in full accord, remember, with the goals of the unit and the organization—then the individual employee goes to work to try to reach them.

In the meantime, the job of the supervisor is to help his people in their efforts to achieve the objectives set. Necessarily, the supervisor has to check from time to time to see how his employee is doing. He does this not in order to police the progress but in order to (1) assure himself as to whether progress is about right, not lagging, and (2) move in as needed, with help, support, assistance, and recognition of his employee's efforts.

A supervisor who waits until the end of the period—say a year after the beginning—is making a serious mistake. By that time, it's too late to help the employee reach his goal. Many personnel people have advocated the once-a-year performance appraisal. The reason is quite obvious why this advocacy is foolish. The time to appraise performance is when it takes place, not months later. It is only when the appraisal is continuing and timely that the appropriate help and support and recognition at each step of the way have real meaning and value.

At the end of the period for which the goal was established, a final review can show whether the goal was actually met. In making this final review, the supervisor needs to take into account:

1. Any change in conditions of enough consequence to affect the goal, either upward or downward. For example, the employee was ill, the seasons were bad, the workload fell off, we got a new machine, etc.

2. Whether the supervisor provided the assistance and support needed, and at the right time. Note that the employee may have some ideas about this!

3. Whether the employee did or did not achieve the goal agreed upon, with due regard for the changing conditions and the supervisor's help. It is well at this point to encourage the employee to discuss his achievement or lack of it. He may provide some very useful insights about the conduct of the work.

For performance substantially exceeding the goals, the supervisor should accord generous recognition. This may mean a bonus, a certificate of merit, a raise, a memo to the personnel file of the individual, depending on circumstances. We need to avoid the business of arguing about a bonus when we are really talking about performance, as noted earlier. We do this by considering the facts of the matter. We can measure the number of services or products achieved, and we can measure the quality of the services or products—always presuming that quality standards are part of the goal itself.

For performance that met the goals set, supervisory congratulations are in order. They should be suitably given and recorded.

For performance that fell below what was reasonable to expect, the supervisor needs to reexamine the goals to be sure that they really were reasonable expectancies. If they were, and it is clear that the employee's work was therefore not up to par, the situation needs to be reviewed carefully and objectively with the employee. It should be pointed out where the slippage seems to have occurred and why. The employee will undoubtedly have some points to bring out here, and they should be carefully evaluated. This discussion is not for the purpose of fixing blame or finding fault, but in order to help the employee improve during the next goal period. This may require more than coaching or counseling; it may require some special training intended to help the employee do better work. And, of course, this sort of thing can take place at any time during the year; it need not wait until the end.

In any event, the employee deserves and should get another

chance. Following the second chance, if the employee is still unable to reach the goal or performance contract set with him, then possibly consideration should be given to placing him in some other kind of work.

SETTING NEW GOALS

Following the first year or goal period, new goals need to be established. These should take into account:

1. Changes in the goals of the organization as a whole, or of the unit in which the employee works.

2. Improvements in technology or working methods that may enable greater achievement or perhaps a different kind, e.g., an electric typewriter, computer operation, easier telephoning, elimination of certain procedural steps or reports.

A pitfall to be avoided, as many studies have shown, is to "up" the goal because the individual exceeded last year's. The impulse to raise the goals is often almost overwhelming, but it is a foolish supervisor who attempts to pressure his outstanding worker into setting higher goals. It sometimes happens that the worker may himself offer to do so, flushed with his success during the previous period. The supervisor will do well to cool this enthusiasm, at least to some extent. Two questions arise: What, indeed, is reasonable to expect? and Is the higher goal fair to the individual if other workers on similar jobs have lower goals?

As in the first goal period, the supervisor proceeds to provide help, support, and encouragement all through the year. He may find, as a matter of fact, that his own experience in supporting his people may provide him with increasing skill in doing it again—and again.

7

Staff Work

OVER THE YEARS many organizations have struggled with the problem of how best to use the services of their staff specialists. The use of staff to full capacity has never been easy to achieve. Sometimes staff specialists are located at headquarters a long way from their supervisors. Sometimes they are located at the same headquarters, but travel schedules being what they are, their supervisors may not be giving them adequate attention. Because of this, staff specialists tend to carry on their work more or less independently of their supervisors. Their work has often been described as technical support, and among these men are the most highly qualified technical experts an organization may have. To a considerable degree, the technical quality of the organization's work is dependent on their specialized knowledge.

The direction and supervision of staff specialists should be the best and most effective possible. To develop a systematic working arrangement between supervisors and their specialists that will result in maximum effectiveness of staff personnel, we need to have a clear picture of what staff specialists are expected to do, how they use their time, and what they accomplish. We may not be able to measure technical advice and counsel directly, but we can at least examine and evaluate the results.

MEANING OF LINE STAFF

By far the majority of government agencies, larger businesses, and sizable companies of the United States are organized in what is known as the line-staff system. This kind of system or structure has been in use for centuries, and is possibly best exemplified in military organizations. Indeed, credit is usually given the military for developing it into an effective working arrangement. There is nothing particularly "scientific" about the line-staff system. It has arisen out of experience, over hundreds of years, and seems to put order and system into large working groups of people. And so it has been used more and more commonly in recent years, even though there are many other ways to group people into working units in an organization.

The definition of line staff in most textbooks goes something like this: The line-staff system is a chain of organization units operating under authority delegated from a central source; and at various points in the organization there are groups of people called staff, whose function is advisory, as distinguished from the line function of command.

This definition is a little obscure, but we can illustrate the essence of a line-staff structure by a simple chart, as in Figure 6.

In this chart a leader is shown directing the work of his little organization. He may issue orders to his two subleaders, who in turn issue orders to their people. The leader is responsible for the workings of the entire organization and he has the authority to see that things get done the way he wants.

The heavy lines indicate the path (or chain) that orders follow, from the leader to his subleaders, and from them to the workers. The heavy lines also show that each subleader is respon-

Figure 6

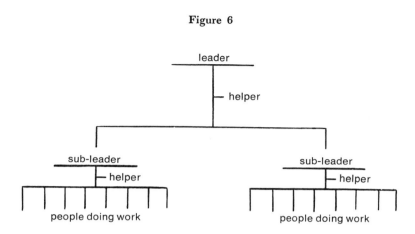

sible for the workings of *his* particular group, and that each one has the necessary authority to see that things get done properly.

Also shown in the chart is a helper for the leader as well as a helper for each of the subleaders. In both cases the helpers are what we call staff people. These staff people issue no orders; they help by giving expert advice or doing highly specialized work. They are not responsible for the workings of the organization, but they are expected to come forward, as needed, with the best possible expert advice and counsel.

Of course, large organizations are much more complex than this. But there is always a leader at the head; there are always staff people who are specialists or experts on various matters, and there are workers who are doing the work the organization is set up to do. We can illustrate a more complex organization by Figure 7.

In this chart we can still see the leader, here called a president though he goes by many names, depending on the custom of the organization. He may be called administrator, chief, governor, commissioner, general superintendent, or by other titles. Very

Figure 7

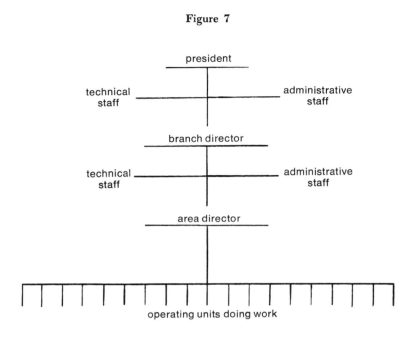

operating units doing work

commonly, the major segments of the organization—shown in the chart as branches—may be headed by a subleader, often called a director, but sometimes known as a superintendent, chief, or by some other appropriate title.

In the chart we can also see the helpers, here called technical staffs or administrative staffs. This chart is still much simplified. In larger organizations these staffs may be quite large and divided into a series of units, each with a special expertise, and headed by a staff leader—for example, a budget director or a chief engineer. These staff leaders may and usually do report to a staff leader who bears an appropriate title, such as vice president or deputy director in charge of administration, or deputy chief for engineering or assistant commissioner for economic analysis. There's no end of titles, most of them intended as much to confer status as to describe functions. Furthermore, titles change about as fashions do. It used to be the thing to do to call the head of a government bureau a *chief*. Now they are generally called *administrators*, and the word chief was downgraded to designate the head of a branch (which is under a *director* of a division, who used also to be a chief).

The line-staff system is in widespread use and is thought by many people to be the "best" system. It is common enough to consider it in general. It has had much success, but it also has some problems that have by no means been solved in many, if not most, organizations. The biggest one of these is the problem of making full use of the services of staff experts. This we come now to consider.

FACTORS DETERMINING STAFF EFFECTIVENESS

To start with we must note that staff people, by definition, have no authority to direct activities, unless it has been specifically delegated to them by their line officer. What this means in a nutshell is that staff people don't give orders. They are expected to give expert advice and counsel, to advocate action to (and in the name of) their supervisor, and to assist him in furthering the job. This type of operation takes skill, just as any other type does, and it is often difficult for some individuals to function successfully on behalf of someone else.

A great deal of emphasis has been placed on this role of the staff officer, and how he must avoid giving orders or usurping the authority of line officers. This emphasis may be deserved, but it is really no more than emphasis on the rules of the game, so to speak. How we win the game is what we are most interested in. Given the rules, what do we do to enable staff people to contribute their fullest efforts to the results we want?

Several points need to be kept in mind as we consider ways to achieve the full effectiveness of staff officials:

▪ What they are to do should be well understood. Putting this another way, the job of any given staff officer should be specific, concrete, and clear.

▪ Since they are expected to give expert advice and counsel, their line officer should demand this of them. Not all line officers are skilled in utilizing such services.

▪ What staff personnel are to do should be well planned and well scheduled. Plans should be specific about work, and how much time will be required for it to be done. The schedules should show when each job is to start and when it is to be completed.

▪ What they do should be recorded and reported, in writing, by some appropriate means. The report should always be available to the staff officer's supervisor, to the staff officer, and to whatever other line and staff officials are involved.

▪ The work they do should be followed up in a systematic way. Usually this "follow-up" is a job for the line officer who is in a position to deal directly with other line officials reporting to him, and to whom he issues orders as needed.

We shall now consider ways to implement these points.

1. The Job of the Staff Specialist

GIVING EXPERT ADVICE AND COUNSEL

This is the first of the two important duties in any staff specialist's job. In this kind of work, it would seem that an economist would offer a different kind of advice than would an engineer. This is true for subject matter. Yet, both such staff specialists, as well as other specialists, need to give their advice and counsel in the same context.

Thus, no staff specialist operates solely in the ivory tower of his specialty—no successful one, that is. His advice, whether economic or hydrologic, has to be geared to the program, policies, and objectives of the organization, and it must be in line with trends, points of emphasis, and operating methods of the organization as a whole. In other words, a specialist's advice must "fit." This is not to say that on occasion a specialist, like anyone else, may not be called on to offer suggestions for improving the organization, suggestions that don't necessarily "fit" at all. With this exception, staff advice and counsel need to be of such a nature as to coincide appropriately with programs, policies, operating methods, and so on. This requirement carries three important corollaries:

The first is that a staff expert must really *be* expert in his field; that is, he must keep up to date professionally.

The second is that a staff expert must also keep up to date on his organization. He must really *know* his organization from top to bottom, be fully familiar with its policies and methods, and understand all the working parts and how they interrelate.

The third is that he must be especially familiar with the area of jurisdiction over which his line officer has control. In this area he must know the strengths and weaknesses of the program with special reference to his particular specialty.

If a staff officer is fully "up" on all these points, he is then in a position to offer advice and counsel, not only to his own line officer, but to any line or staff officials operating under that officer.

These three items are of critical importance. A staff expert who is out of date is possibly worse than no expert at all. One who really doesn't know and understand his organization, especially the segment in which he operates, is likely to go about fouling things up without realizing it. There is nothing so terrifying as ignorance in action.

HELPING GET THE JOB DONE

In this second important duty, our staff specialist helps his supervisor by inventorying, planning, scheduling, and completing certain jobs—in his particular specialty—that need to get done.

Inventory: The intent is to move things forward in the

geographical or functional area involved, from where they are to where they ought to be. In turn, this means that any staff specialist must be fully informed on the status of his specialty in each of the organizational units he serves (as noted in the third corollary above).

Obviously, some units, areas, branches, states, or regions will require more attention; some will require less. Some units will be well advanced in his specialty; some may be lagging. There is no point in lavishing efforts on units that are in satisfactory operation. Better to concentrate on bringing up the laggers.

Any supervisor of a staff specialist must assure himself that his specialist is up to date on the situation in each of the organizational units he serves. This is an important point. It is easy to get out of date on the work of a unit the specialist hasn't seen for some time. Unless the inventory is up to date and factually correct, faulty planning and time distribution can very easily result.

One useful way for preparing a concise, clearly delineated inventory is to prepare it on the basis of some format such as the following (using a columnar spread sheet for convenience). In Figure 8 we are using an engineer, but we could use any other kind of technical or administrative specialist. All we have to do in the chart is to list the specific problems that must be given attention in whatever field of expertise we are interested.

Here are listed nine important problems which should be the things to which our staff engineer devotes his major attention. In a sense, each one is a project to be worked on. It is easy to see that in this case our engineer obviously ought to spend most time in Units C and D, and that he must also get at the design problem in Unit B.

Planning and Scheduling: There are, of course, a number of well-known ways to draw up a plan of action. In a nutshell, what the specialist and his supervisor must do is to agree specifically on what the specialist needs to do in the year or even years ahead. The inventory worked out above carries much information of value in preparing a plan, but it is not enough in itself. The

Figure 8

Specific Problem	Unit A	Unit B	Unit C	Unit D	Other units where the specialist must work
1. Designing dams	√	—	—	—	
2. Spillways	+	+	—	+	
3. Etc.	√	√	√	—	
4. Etc.	√	+	√	√	
5. Etc.	√	+	—	—	
6. Adequacy of technical guides in use	+	+	√	√	
7. Adequacy of plans	√	+	—	√	
8. Quality of engineering work	√	+	—	—	
9. General acceptance of engineering advice	+	+	—	√	

+ = Outstanding   √ = Satisfactory   — = Below what's needed

business of simply "spending time" in certain offices is exactly where staff operation is often weak.

What we need at this point, in addition to the showing of the inventory, is (1) a clearcut description or understanding of the problem so that both the supervisor and his specialist are clear about its nature; (2) a specific agreement on the approach most likely to effect a solution, and (3) an estimate in man-days of the time required for the job plus an estimated completion date. These three points are sometimes difficult to work out, but they are essential if the specialist is to make his efforts really count. In a sense, this adds up to an analysis of work load, which any worker needs to have in mind as he approaches his job.

To illustrate how this might work, let us suppose that a line supervisor asks his engineer—the one who made the inventory—to take a sheet of paper and list the three points for each problem. It could be done (it has been done in some offices) by using one sheet of paper for each of the nine problems shown on the inventory example, thus:

PROBLEM: (A brief description of the situation and why there is a problem in need of solution.)

APPROACHES: (A brief outline of the best approach to a solution in each of the offices shown in the inventory as needing help. The approach in one unit may well be different from that in another.)

ESTIMATED TIME: (Here our specialist judges the approximate number of man-days he will have to spend to get the job done. He bases this on experience. He may not be able to devote all the required man-days in one month; the days may have to be distributed according to season and/or other demands. He puts a final completion date here, also estimated.)

This simple assembly of information can make the discussions between the specialist and his supervisor quite factual and specific. Where the number of problems is large, and the estimated time required is also large, an assignment of priorities may help in arranging an order agreeable to both supervisor and specialist.

Furthermore, if the estimated cost appears out of all reason for the benefits expected, the supervisor or manager may want to get some further facts or information before he decides to okay the plans. Why does this sort of thing cost so much? Is it materials or labor? Is it possibly a procedure that could be simplified? Such questions may prove to be illuminating from time to time, and the staff specialist should be required—and prepared—to answer them.

Incidentally, these problem sheets should be kept on hand for later review. They are collectively a plan of action, and comparisons can be made later between what was planned and estimated and what was actually accomplished. There ought to be good reasons for changing approaches, time estimates, and completion dates.

It is a relatively simple matter to place the planned items in a schedule, showing by appropriate dates where the specialist will be and what he will be doing. There are a number of ways to do this; which one is used is largely a matter of choice. One good method is to use a calendar with small numbers in the blocks, and plenty of space in each block for writing.

The schedule is built as far ahead as is practical. Some people keep it about a year ahead, with the immediate three to six months more closely scheduled than the later months. However this is done, a copy should be available both to the specialist and his supervisor.

2. Reporting

When a staff specialist finishes his work at an office, he needs to prepare a brief report of what he did, and any agreed-upon actions to be taken by the office and by him. This report ought to be signed or initialed by the responsible line official at the office to indicate his agreement. A copy of the report stays at the office, the specialist keeps one for himself, and his supervisor gets one.

These reports are variously known as trip reports, staff reports, etc., but the point is that unless actions and agreements on further action are committed to writing, they can very easily be forgotten or "mis-remembered." The only valid reason for making no report is that nothing happened worth reporting—an assumption many people make when no report is forthcoming.

3. Follow-Up

As line officers receive staff reports or trip reports of the sort described above, they are in a position to take action. It is not enough that the staff specialist and the field office line official agreed upon further actions. Our line official must now confirm this—and let us remember that, so far, there has been no exercise of authority by anyone, since the staff specialist cannot issue orders. Now, however, if the line officer nearest to the specialist agrees with the recommended actions, he so advises the line officer of the field office. He may also set some deadlines and require a completion report. And he should not then forget the matter. He—or his secretary if he has one—must maintain a tickler file that will turn up the report again on the deadline date. The whole matter is relentlessly pursued until the actions wanted are complete.

4. Completion of Plans

There remains the matter of determining whether the plans made by the specialist were actually carried out as planned. This is not a matter of checking up on the specialist. Rather it is a review of the way the problems or projects came out, whether the time estimate was valid, and whether the completion date turned out to be realistic—all this in order to assist the specialist in distributing his time better and to enable him to improve his planning the next time. Unless this review is made, there is really no way of ascertaining whether the plans and accompanying schedules—on which a great deal depends—were valid, and whether new ones are likely to be any better.

Another point is also important in this completion action: If the estimates of the man-days required for each problem or project turned out to be about right, we then have a validated basis for further planning. We also are able to begin stating with confidence based on facts whether the specialist job is adequately filled with one man or whether two or more are required. This is something that perennially has had to be estimated, based on people's beliefs. And, as everyone knows, judgment as to the number of staff people required in any given situation varies with the people judging. There are frequent wide differences of opinion on staffing, especially between staff specialists and line officials. When we can compare what it actually did take to complete a given project, in man-days, with what was estimated, there is likely to be less argument over the number of staff people required to perform a given function.

From this it is clear that our staff specialist must keep track of the time he spends on his various problems or projects. This can be done by means of a diary or other notebook. *All* the time spent on a given project needs to be noted. This will include time spent preparing for field work, time on any study required in preparation, time in the field office, preparing the report, and so on. By the time the problem or project is completed, it should be possible to summarize the time it took to do it. If the plans of action are for a year ahead, then such a summary could be prepared annually. To keep things in reasonable order, the specialist may wish to make notes of man-days actually used on a project on the planning sheet discussed earlier. From this he can easily prepare a final summary at the end of the year. Such a summary, arrayed on a spread sheet, might look like Table 2.

TABLE 2

Problem	MAN-DAYS Estimated	Actual
1	40	34
2	16	10
3	12	10
4	—	—
5	20	21
6	—	—
7	10	6
8	20	18
9	10	8
Total	128	107

Two points are obvious in this hypothetical example (keyed to the inventory in Figure 8):

The first is that the estimates were generally too large. This suggests a little tighter planning and scheduling may enable our specialist to get more done next year.

The second is that there are 260 man-days in a year, of which only 107 are accounted for here, leaving a balance of 153. We cannot say at once whether this is good or bad. We have already noted that staff specialists have the duty of keeping abreast of their special field. Some of this may be done at home, but some is done in the office, at meetings, visits to research stations, and the like.

Time must be allotted for this admittedly important activity. Furthermore, any specialist has certain general administrative work to perform such as attending staff meetings, making plans and schedules, writing letters, preparing special reports, serving on committees, and the like. This takes time and is important.

The alert manager will see at once that, if the primary reason for having a staff specialist is problem-solving, then excessive time spent on keeping abreast and especially on general administration must be guarded against. That is, we cannot afford to eat up the specialist's time in activities that may prevent him from performing fully in his specialty.

Staff experts are quite likely to resist or even to resent this type of operation. Engineers generally are probably an exception to this statement; they are, by training, systematic in their attack on problems.

But many experts simply do not see themselves being bound by such a process. Two points suggest themselves in dealing with such resistance: (1) convince the staff expert that his expertise is needed badly and here is one way to get it fully into use, and (2) here is a way to get their expertise into operation, with the full cooperation of the line officials involved. This last point is an important one; few experts believe that their advice and counsel bears much fruit. A little experience in not having their recommendations considered, and they will embrace a system designed to implement their efforts.

The job of the staff specialist is not an easy one at best. His accomplishments must be measured largely by actions other people take because of his ideas. But it seems clear that the more systematic he and his supervisors are in approaching his work, the more efficient and productive his efforts are likely to be. The basic ideas suggested in this simple system of operation are not new. They have to do with getting the problems listed, defined, evaluated, and recorded, and with estimating and reviewing their cost in terms of man-days of work. The end result of such a system, as tested and proven in a number of organizations, is increased efficiency and productivity.

8

Communications Systems

No ORGANIZATION is likely to survive without an effective system of internal communications. It is now generally accepted that the people composing an organization must be kept currently informed on such major matters as these:

- What the organization stands for, as expressed in
    Its objective or purpose
    Its general policies, organization, structure, and
        operating procedures
    Its plans for the future, both immediate and long-term
- How the organization is doing, as expressed in or by
    Its activities
    Its progress
    Its accomplishments or results being achieved

It is clear that information about what the organization stands for must come from the headquarters office. In whatever way the objectives, policies, programs, and plans are formulated, they must be sent out from a common center, and they ought to bear the approval of the directing head of the organization. It is equally clear that information concerning how the organization is doing must flow from the outlying units or groups of workers to the headquarters offices.

These two processes are often called "downward" communications and "upward" communications. Actually, of course, the conveying of information goes from person to person or office to office, not up and not down. At any rate, what we need to concern ourselves with equally is (1) the flow of information from the central managing office of an organization to all its people, and (2) the flow of information from all the people in an organization to its central managing group. If both these processes are well handled, every member of the organization has the opportunity to be well and currently informed.

Unfortunately, the need for both outflowing and inflowing streams of information is not always fully understood. Many managers and executives think of communications largely or entirely in terms of the outflowing stream. Their intent is to get the people informed about what the central managing office wants. This idea is good, of course, as far as it goes. The trouble is, however, that it goes only halfway. One-way communication has been shown in many studies to be deficient both between people and between the offices or units of an organization. It might almost be said that there is no such thing as effective one-way communication. Either it is two-way or it is nothing.

A particularly good statement of the values of inflowing information, or "upward" communication, has been expressed by offices of the Johnson & Johnson Company of New Brunswick, New Jersey:

"There are many values that accrue to those managers who listen willingly, who urge their subordinates to talk freely and honestly. Upward communication reveals to them the degree to which ideas passed down are accepted. In addition, it stimulates employees to participate in the operation of their department or unit, and therefore, encourages them to defend the decisions and support the policies cooperatively developed with management.

The opportunity for upward communication also encourages employees to contribute valuable ideas for improving departmental or company efficiency. Finally, it is through upward communication that executives learn, in time to avert them, the many explosive situations which arise daily in industry."[1]

Managers of government agencies should have no difficulty in utilizing this statement of an industrial organization. It applies almost directly to the operation of government departments and bureaus, indeed to almost any kind of organization.

A CLIMATE FOR COMMUNICATIONS

We consider next how communications may be systematized, both the outflowing or "downward" kind, and the inflowing or "upward" kind. But first let us consider the climate in which both kinds operate most effectively. Characteristics of this climate may be identified as follows:

■ There must be a full and clear understanding on the part of the executive head, as well as his immediate major assistants, of the great value and pervasive influence of communications among all the people of his organization.

■ There must be an equally clear understanding on the part of every supervisor, no matter how near or far his location from the central headquarters, that communications are of key importance and that one of his primary supervisory functions is to facilitate them, both "upward" and "downward." This must include the practice by all supervisors of effective oral and written presentation of ideas, *and* of sympathetic listening and perceptive reading. Supervisors can be trained in these skills.[2]

Basically, it must be remembered also that a message is simply not transmitted unless it is received. (1) It must be under-

1. *A Project in Executive Development,* by Earl G. Planty and William V. Machaver, of Johnson & Johnson, New Brunswick, New Jersey; reprinted (mimeographed) by the USDA Graduate School, 1961.
2. See *The Successful Supervisor,* by William R. Van Dersal (3rd ed., New York: Harper & Row, Publishers, 1974), pp. 112–31.

stood, (2) it must come from a reliable source, and (3) the receiver must be in a position to do something about it.

■ In addition to the managerial and supervisory force, every other person in the organization must also see and understand the need for intercommunication among all members and segments of the agency or company.

■ Finally, no person should be afraid to speak his piece, and everyone should be encouraged to speak it. The administrative atmosphere should be such that this is easy to achieve.

OUTFLOWING INFORMATION

Before we examine the basic elements of a system for passing information from headquarters to all outlying units or offices, it may be worthwhile to review briefly the problems faced:

Each supervisor, regardless of his location in the organization, must keep his people informed. He, in turn, must be kept informed by *his* supervisor, who must be kept current by the man who supervises him, and so on. All this can be done orally. But when an organization becomes large, the passing on of information by word of mouth begins to take too long and gets quite cumbersome. Also, the information may become considerably changed as it is relayed from one individual or group to the next. Hence, it becomes necessary to put such information in more permanent from, that is, in writing, to which all concerned can refer to be sure their understanding is correct. Written or printed information of this kind, intended for all the people in an organization, is usually developed in the form of official memorandums, manuals, or handbooks. These are organized in appropriate ways, and kept up to date by additions, deletions, changes, and so on.

In a large organization the official collections of memorandums, manual material, or handbook material may get quite large. There is a need for indexing, cross-references, and the like, to guide the users. This usually means that certain people must devote time to the preparation, distribution, indexing, updating, and filing of such materials on the basis of some kind of system. As the material grows, many of the people in the organization begin to feel hopeless about it. The larger the manuals, the more people tend to ignore them. "Experts" emerge who know what all the rules and regulations are and where to find them. The rest of the people rely either on the "experts," or they tend to take action based on what they consider to be common sense. Sometimes this "common sense" fits into organizational philosophy, but sometimes it does not.

None of this is new. Organizations have been faced with the need for achieving understanding by all their people for a long time. All sorts of arrangements have been devised to do this. But reviews of many such arrangements lead to the inescapable conclusion that the objective of such systems is commonly forgotten. Materials are often sent out in such volume as to overwhelm the users. Some subjects are fully treated; on others the system is silent. Distribution is often inadequate: many people may receive information of no value in their work; some people may fail to get information they really need. The reading level of the written material is usually far higher than the reading ability of the people; as a consequence understanding is the more difficult to achieve. No provision whatever may be made for "feedback" to determine whether all the people understand clearly what the written material is intended to convey. And so on.

In what follows a series of ideas is proposed that can assist an executive either in the development of a communications system or in the evaluation of the one he uses.

1. A System of Issuances

The heart of any system of issuances is the written material that expresses the continuing instructions of the organization. This kind of material is important enough to be referred to by the people or various segments of the entire organization for a long time, that is, on a continuing basis. It may be issued in simple memorandum form, or it may be printed in a special format for inclusion in a manual of some sort. But, however it is issued, it contains only those instructions that remain constantly in force and effect. Obviously this instructional or manual series will be modified from time to time as required. Changes will ordinarily be few and far between except in a rapidly developing or expanding organization.

All other informational material should be issued in some other form. This will consist largely of temporary instructions, announcements, transmittals, and the like. The temporary material may be called advisories or notices, or designated by some other title that clearly separates it from the lasting or continuing instructions. Advisories may be destroyed after they have achieved their purpose of conveying information.

Thus we have two series of issuance, one that contains information of use over a long period—the manual; and one that is temporary in character—the advisory.

It should be noted in passing that the two series are not separated on the basis of policy versus procedure. It is rarely possible to separate policy from procedure. Procedures are, in themselves, expressions of policy. Few policies are issued without procedural instructions intended to implement them. The manual and advisory series are separated on the question of whether the material needs to be referred to for an indefinite period or only for a short time.

There are five important ideas concerning the lasting Manual or Instructional series. All these are based on the fact that the instructions are important enough to remain in effect indefinitely, or until changed. The ideas are these:

Drafts: A draft of the material should always be sent to or discussed with line officials in the organization to determine whether they are generally in agreement with the subject matter. Some of them will agree entirely; some will suggest minor changes; some may suggest major ones. Their suggestions are given careful consideration, and are used in preparing the final draft.

All this presumes that the line officers are in substantial agreement with the proposed instruction. If it should turn out that most of them consider the instruction unwise, the matter had better be reviewed. They may be right, or they may have misunderstood. In either case, the instruction needs overhauling. After all, these line officers must see that continuing instructions are followed.

The practice of referring first drafts of issuances to line officials affected is an important one. It provides for their participation, and it informs them well before any action need be taken. It avoids the element of surprise, and it enables the line officials to play a part in and contribute to the development of important matters in the organization. In this discussion we consider all supervisors to be line officials.

Readability: Our second corollary is that the material must be comfortable and easy reading for all the people who must use it. There are various well-known ways of assuring this ease of reading. Newspapers and popular magazines make use of these means to be sure their material is reaching the largest possible audience.[3]

If most or indeed only some, of those who must read the material have an 8th grade reading ability, then the material must be written for ease of reading by 8th grade graduates. If the material is comfortable reading only for college graduates, then any of the people in the organization who lack that much education are likely to have difficulty reading and understanding it. Worse, if the material is not comfortable reading even for college graduates—and this is possibly the commonest situation of all —then almost no one at all will find it easy to understand.

To follow through on this idea, someone must review all

3. Gunning's Fog Index is a simple one to use; so is Flesch's Reading Ease. The first is explained in the *Technique of Clear Writing*, by Robert Gunning (New York: McGraw-Hill, Inc., 1952). The second is described in *The Art of Readable Writing*, by Rudolf Flesch. (New York: Harper & Row, 1949).

instructional or manual material for the reading level required. Such an editor must work closely with the originators of the material. This, obviously, takes a little time. It may take several days to do it for a sizable issuance. The originators will complain. They will point to the urgency for getting out the instructions. They will argue that certain phraseology is sacred, no matter how badly it expresses an idea. They will condemn the unfortunate editor. But the question is whether it is worthwhile to spend a little extra time making permanent instructions clear. Instructions that are not clear and easy to read can cause a great deal of misunderstanding. All this can waste many man-*years* of time in a large organization.

Formal Issuance: Presuming our instructional material has been fully reviewed and edited for ease of reading, it is now nearly ready for formal or official issuance. This had better be done by the executive head of the organization. He, and he alone, should sign it, or by other means signify that this is his instruction to the organization. And before he gives his approval, he had better be sure it says what he wants. His whole organization is going to live by this instruction, and all his people will expect him to live by it also.

Centralizing approval in the executive head of the organization provides an important means of coordination. It provides for organization-wide instructions. It blocks the staff officer who is overly anxious to put out instructions on his own hook that may not coincide as well as might be with existing instructions. And it gives authority to the instructions because they are personally issued by the head of the organization.

Distribution and Filing: Our fourth idea has to do with arrangements for distributing and filing the material. These arrangements are properly part of the system decided upon well in advance. In a nutshell, the copies should carry on their face a listing of the offices or officials to whom the instructions are sent, and a descriptive coding of some sort that tells all recipients where to place or file them.

Distribution of instructions may not always be to all personnel or to all offices. Sometimes they may go only to budget or other staff offices, or to branch offices, or some other segment of the organization. This should be made clear on the face of the material.

Filing of instructions is important. Receiving offices ought to be able to file them in some system that enables ready reference. For example, if an organization expects to issue instructions on sales, or on battleships, then the filing system should contain such categories. Whether the material is put in three-ring binders or some other kind of file, issuance designations should coincide with filling designations. All this makes for ease of handling and use on the receiving end.

Discussion: Our fifth and last idea is that written instructions of special importance should be discussed fully with the receivers by informed officials. Despite the utmost care in preparation, written materials can still be misunderstood or misinterpreted. A series of conferences intended to bring about full understanding may sometimes be required. After all, if the directing executive of an organization wants his instructions understood, he had better make use of more than one means of communication.

2. *The President's Letter*

The head of an organization must have a means of keeping in touch with all the people in his organization. This means is usually informal in character, but it should be an expression of the executive head, and, if it is in writing, it should be signed by him. It should be issued at frequent, but not necessarily regular, intervals. And it should be a simple and direct reflection of the man directing the organization.

House organs, as commonly used, simply cannot substitute for the president's letter, as described above. Furthermore, repeated surveys of the value of house organs indicate clearly that their value is, to say the least, questionable. Commonly enough, house organs are printed on slick paper, full of photos of employees getting awards, safety slogans, jokes, personals, and the like. By and large, as it turns out in survey after survey, the employees couldn't care less. On the other hand, surveys do indicate that a direct letter from the head of the organization is valued above most other things the employees get.

One of the best of these president's letters is a simple, multi-lithed sheet, signed by the president and containing information the employees need to know. It's not issued regularly, because if it is, there's often need for filler. It's issued when the president has enough copy for two sides of a single sheet, or when he's anxious to get out something that can't wait. He writes part—or all of it—himself, and he lets only those things he considers important get into it. In the truest possible sense, the letter is a projection of his personality. If, in this letter, the president deals honestly and sincerely with his people and in a timely way, the employees await its issuance with real interest. It's a good idea if the president's letter is on paper of a distinctive color—but no special format is required. Incidentally, because of its simplicity, the president's letter can be relatively inexpensive.

Plenty of people may contribute to this letter, but the items that get into it should get there because the president thinks they're important and wants to use them. This is where the president tells his people what's going on, what's coming up, what's important to the organization—that is, to the people—and how he feels about things. He uses it as though he were talking in a friendly and direct way with each person working in the organization he heads.

INFLOWING INFORMATION

As we have already noted, the flow of information from the people to the central headquarters ranks equally in importance with the outflow of information from the central office to the people. This is the so-called "upward" communication that has been receiving considerable emphasis in the literature of management in recent years. The question is: How does it best take place, and how may it be usefully systematized?

1. Formal Reports

Normally, in any sizable organization, there is some kind of a reporting system. With specified regularity, reports are sent to supervising offices from places where work is going on. If there are a number of "levels"—and there almost always are—the reports are usually consolidated, digested, and passed on from one "level" to the next. Eventually the directing head of the organization gets his copies. Some such reporting system as this is generally agreed to be necessary to the operation of any government agency, company, or industry.

The elements of such a system seem simple enough but reporting systems in general, both in government and industry, tend to suffer from many ailments. Possibly the worst of these is that the reporting systems tend to uncontrolled growth. It is all too easy to add "just one more" item to the report; after all, "they have to make it anyway, and this won't make that much difference." But, of course, it is the total of such single items that may eventually create a staggering burden for the offices or units that must initiate a report. Both government agencies and businesses are afflicted by the overburden of reporting. Neither is immune, and the cost of such poor systems can be very high.

In some cases, of course, the gaps in a reporting system may be much worse than their total burden. Exactly what the reporting system should carry can be specified only for each particular organization. Incidentally, it had better be specified for each kind of report, since duplication between reports can lead directly to further overburdening.

A REPORTS INVENTORY

To deal with this matter of reports, several issues need to be considered:

1. How many and what kinds of reports there are presently, in the company or organization. If your organization hasn't made a complete check on reports before, you are likely to be a little startled at the results of such an inventory. In businesses and agencies that have been operating for very many years, the proliferation is often astounding. An inventory can show what the situation really is. It must take into account a number of matters that usually do not appear until a count is attempted.

2. Someone has to define "reports." There's a difference between reports required regularly and reports that are asked for once or only occasionally. For example, an accident report is occasional; it's made only when there's an accident. On the other hand, a monthly report on safety meetings is a regular report.

3. What a report is also depends on who's looking at it. For example, a report required of 100 offices every month amounts to $100 \times 12 = 1,200$ reports each year. There is a cost of making one of these, in each office; the total cost of preparation is the single unit cost multiplied by 1,200. The executive head may think he gets only one report, but if it comes from 100 offices, he is really talking about 1,200 reports a year—from the point of view of the originating offices. This has to be considered in any inventory.

Once we know how many reports there are, *in total*, as well as how many *kinds* of reports, then we can consider the three key questions:

▪ Do we need every item carried by each kind of report? Indeed, this may lead to the question: Do we need this report at all? We used to; do we still have to have it?

▪ Do we need items not carried by each of the present kinds of reports?

▪ Is there any other way to get the information we need at a cost less than that of each of the various kinds of reports, considering the cost of the total number of individual reports necessary for the single final report?

The making of an inventory of reports and the analysis that

should accompany it are likely to cause something of a stir in many organizations. Regular reports, even simple ones, may be found to be far more expensive than anyone imagined. There is quite likely to be a reaction: let's cut down the number, eliminate duplications, cut out the old ones no longer serving a purpose, etc. This reaction is quite natural, although it can easily result in throwing the baby away with the bath. What we need to do, actually, after the shakedown cruise of the inventory, is to develop some system for managing all the reports that are really needed. This system will require some person or persons to develop it and see that it works on a continuing basis.

One simple approach to reports control is for the executive head of the organization, or for designated, authorized line officials (not staff units) to require anyone who wants a report to set forth, in detail, the following kinds of information:

■ The name and contents of the proposed report, together with a sample. If a form is to be used, it should be shown.

■ The frequency of the report, that is, how often it will need to be made.

■ The number of offices, units, or people who will need to prepare it; and the number of places where it may be consolidated.

■ The uses to be made of the material in the report, with clear, justifying statements supporting every item.

■ The costs involved, including time spent on collection and preparation of data, typing, mailing, filing of extra copies, distribution, consolidations, time of studying on the receiving end, etc.

■ A place for the approving officer to sign. Here he certifies that the need for the report is commensurate with its cost. He then becomes responsible for the new report.

If such information as this is filed in the central headquarters office, then it is possible to manage the reporting system. Only properly authorized reports should be permitted to circulate; wildcat reports should be stopped. Lastly, it will pay an organization to review this reports file every so often. The world moves on and things change. So should reports.

2. Less Formal Reporting

A formal reporting system, of the sort described above, can be of great service, but it cannot serve every purpose. Most importantly it cannot ordinarily reveal the opinions, beliefs, understanding, or judgments of the personnel of the organization. These opinions and judgments are quite available; every employee, so to speak, is a ready source. The question is how to get them together so that they can have meaning to the executive or managing heads of the organization.

We have already pointed to one means to use in discovering the feelings of the people of the agency or company. In issuing instructions, we noted that we need to find out how the subject matter will strike the organization as a whole. Will it be clear to the readers? Will it be misunderstood in whole or in part? Will it cover all situations as it should? Is it, on the whole, readily acceptable to the personnel and considered generally to be a good thing, a progressive step forward? Let us note in passing that there are usually people in the headquarters offices who feel they can answer these questions easily. But this is not always true. Correctly, the people who can answer them are all the people in the organization who will be affected. *They* must be asked, and it is well to ask before an issuance goes into effect. Otherwise a good deal of trouble can develop very easily.

The foregoing paragraph repeats what has already been said, but the repetition seems justified. Your people are either for you or they are against you, or worse, they are indifferent. The attitudes and loyalties of your people are of great importance. They can make or break the organization. In a very systematic and regular way, therefore, we need to be sure how they react—to objectives, to programs, to plans for the future. It is the people of an organization who meet the deadlines, enable the organization to reach its objectives, develop the program, carry out the plans. Favorable attitudes engendered by enlightened administrative practice can have a major effect on company or agency success.[4]

With such ideas in mind, it becomes obvious that all those situations in which a supervisor or manager meets and talks with his people can become collecting points for information of value in directing the operations of the organization. As supervisory personnel learn how to listen so that their understanding approaches as closely as possible that of their people, then we begin to perceive how the interests of the organization and of its people may be made to coincide.

The discussion situations include such things as staff meetings (in the general sense), committee, task force, or syndicate meetings, individual counseling between supervisors and their people, workshops, training sessions of all sorts, conferences, informal or formal grievance meetings, and so on. Such meetings are fruitful places to get ideas, always provided the supervising or managing officials are as willing to listen as they are to talk. It follows that supervisors need to conduct whatever meetings they need in some regular way. It is seldom that an effective supervisor, no matter where he may be placed in an organization, can be fully successful without meeting with his people at regular intervals, say once a month or whatever other period is practical.

Key to all this is the belief—expressed in action—of the executive head of the organization that he wants and needs the participation of all his people in furthering the purposes and operation of his agency or company. This attitude, like the rain soaking into soil, will soon permeate the actions of all managerial and supervisory personnel. This is the reason an executive had better look to himself if he wants "upward" communication.

4. To gain a clearer understanding of this philosophy, I recommend very careful study of *New Patterns of Management*, by Rensis Likert (New York: McGraw-Hill, Inc., 1961). In addition, see Douglas McGregor's book, *The Human Side of Enterprise* (New York: McGraw-Hill, Inc., 1960) and Alfred Marrow's *The Failure of Success* (New York: Amacom, 1972).

THE GRAPEVINE

Many managers and executives deplore the grapevine. They would suppress it if they could. They become angry when a rumor flies through their organization. They tend to blame their people, or at least certain ones whom they consider to be gossips. They feel that "people do too much loose talking." They would feel happier if their people did not talk among themselves about the company or the agency they head.

But the grapevine will always be with us. Wherever two or more people work together, they are bound to talk with each other about what they are doing and how they feel about it. This is about as natural as anything we humans do. And it is certainly not something that can be stopped by any ordinary means. In prisons where there may be heavy penalties for talking, penalties that are harshly enforced, men nevertheless manage to convey ideas and information back and forth. In industries where talking has been forbidden among workers on the theory that it detracts from productivity, people still find ways of communicating. In schoolrooms where pupils may not talk or whisper to each other—remember?—they find ways of communicating with each other. In communities where people were punished for gossiping—as in early Colonial America—people nevertheless gossiped.

So, without question, the grapevine will always be with us. It would be wiser to recognize this as a fact. And it would seem only sensible to utilize the grapevine as one of the environmental conditions of management and supervision. Indeed, if people are not interested enough in the work they do to talk about it, then possibly the lack of such a grapevine is an indicator of something seriously wrong in the organization.

Now, what do we know about the grapevine?

1. Where two or more people are together they form a connection in the grapevine. This depends on an opportunity. The

opportunity may be in an office, at the watercooler, in the halls, in the restrooms, at lunch or coffee breaks, on the telephone, going to and from work, over the back fence, at bridge parties, or in correspondence.

2. Some people tend to move from one group to another to carry news, rumors, or hearsay. Some people do not. Everyone, almost without exception, will listen, even though he may not pass information along

3. The accuracy of information passed from one person to another—that is, of the grapevine itself—is uncertain. Sometimes the information may be quite correct. Sometimes it may be incorrect.

4. Something dramatic, or surprising, or considered to be highly important tends to be passed along most rapidly.

5. Secrecy tends to add spice to information. It also tends to create false information to be carried on the grapevine. This is because people will speculate about secret material and, as they talk, pass their suspicions along on the grapevine.

6. The grapevine usually consists of oral information; it is less often written, as in letters.

7. Even so, distance is not necessarily a controlling factor in the operation of the grapevine. Telephones and present-day speed of travel make it possible for rumors to span the continent in a matter of hours, if not minutes.

8. Grapevine connections often depend on friends or acquaintances, less commonly on total strangers.

9. Some people think they gain added prestige by appearing to know something others do not. They may exaggerate to get this effect, and they pass their exaggerations along to others.

10. When people are anxious or uncertain about their relation to company or agency action, almost all will seek to learn what others may know, and some will voice and pass on their uneasy feelings plus their suspicions respecting events likely (they think) to happen.

11. Some people will plant rumors on the grapevine to see

what happens. They are amused at its workings. Sometimes these rumors force managing officials to affirm or deny them.

12. Relatively few people will make a real effort to check the accuracy of the information passed over the grapevine. This is the idle gossip idea. Supervisors ordinarily will check the accuracy especially when they consider the information important to them and their groups.

With the foregoing ideas in mind, we may next consider how best to deal with the grapevine, remembering that it will always be active whether we like it or not. We might consider the following points:

- If it is natural—and indeed desirable—for people to talk about their work, then if correct and timely information is always widely and easily available, the grapevine will tend to carry correct, rather than incorrect, information.

- When the executives of the organization do not wish information to be released, they face a dilemma. Information known to two or only a few people is not secret. A secret can reside only in a single person, not in several. A secret revealed to anyone at all is no longer a secret.

The filling of a position, the transfer of a group of people to another city, an important change in policy or organization, and similar matters, often take time to work out. During the time required to mature the plans, people are going to talk. Lacking correct information—which may, in fact, not even be clear to the executives contemplating the change—they will speculate, fill in the gaps in their knowledge, and pass the word along.

During the inevitable time lag in such situation, the final decisions can scarcely be released until they are indeed final. However, a great deal of information can be released. The *fact* that the company or agency is studying the qualifications of a number of able men, and that it will announce its decision in a few weeks, can be explained. The *fact* that action has to be taken about a policy that isn't working very well can be explained and discussed. The *fact* that the company or agency must reorganize, plus the *fact* that the solution to the problem requires that the people of the organization stay within it, either in old or new capacities, can be explained. If the grapevine is provided with these facts, or if passage over it is forestalled by public, widespread announcements, then management has much less to fear.

▪ Since the grapevine carries information that people believe to be important enough to talk about, it is important for managing officials to listen to it. When they discover erroneous or inaccurate information being passed along, they need to take steps to correct that information. If they do not, no one else will. This is something that all supervisors must be alert to.

SUMMARY

Let us now summarize the elements of a communications system.

Outflowing Information: This includes several elements:

▪ A system of issuances originating in headquarters offices consisting of (*a*) permanent or continuing instructions, often put in a well-indexed manual, and (*b*) temporary or advisory notices that may be destroyed after reading.

▪ A series of regular or special conferences to be sure people understand instructions and especially important or major matters.

▪ A simple letter issued by the executive head to all the people in his organization, not necessarily regular, but frequent enough to keep current information flowing.

Inflowing information: This includes:

▪ A formal reporting system carrying information on how each office is doing. The information may be separated into statistical reports and narrative reports, or the two may be combined. *Each report* should be evaluated before being approved for use, considering all costs and benefits, content, need, best periodicity, etc. *All reports* should be reviewed about every 3 to 5 years to be sure they are still needed, carry all information needed and none not needed, could be eliminated, combined with others, expanded, etc.

▪ Less formal reporting, generally by supervisors, originating from conferences, staff meetings, special events, and other useful gatherings.

Obviously, these few elements are only a skeleton of a communications system. There may well be a need to elaborate one or most of them. But the perceptive manager will do well to keep his system as simple as he can. It's easier to use, faster to operate, and more efficient when it's simple than when it's complex.

9

Reports and Reporting

THERE IS A VERY OLD STORY of a soldier in a remote installation who was fed up with his assignment and bored with life in general. One day, as he was staring vacantly at the ceiling in his office, he noticed a spiral twist of sticky flypaper hung there to catch insects. Vaguely interested, he counted the flies on the twisted paper, then on several others hanging about the quarters. On impulse he seized paper and pen and wrote up a Flypaper Report. He solemnly noted the number of flies per twisted ribbon, the number per linear foot, subtotals, and the total number of flies captured as of that date. He typed this up and sent it on "up the line" as a practical joke.

Somewhat to his disappointment, nothing happened. So, a month later he sent in another report headed "Monthly Flypaper Report." He kept this up for several months, taking secret delight in what must be happening at headquarters. But still nothing. Finally he lost interest and relapsed into his boredom. Ten days after the close of the month, he received a curt notice: "Your

Monthly Flypaper Report is now 10 days overdue. Send latest report forward immediately."

This foolish story may or may not be true. But it is often told, and it says a number of things about reports:

- Reports are often not really needed.
- Receiving offices frequently do not read the reports they require.
- People get into a habit of getting or making reports, become accustomed to them, and become uneasy if they aren't received "as usual" on time.
- "Wildcat" reports can be started by almost anyone.
- Some reports carry information of little or no value.

—and yet, a good reporting system can be the lifeblood of an organization.

It is, in fact, generally recognized that reports are an essential tool in the operation of a company or agency. If there is a high degree of decentralization, reports become that much more important. Wherever one unit or office needs to know what others are doing, some kind of report is required. Obviously, the directing head of a national organization, or the branch or area or regional heads, must all be kept fully aware of what is going on in the offices or units under their jurisdiction.

Besides this internal need, reports must be made from time to time to offices or agencies outside the organization. Indeed, numerous organizations are in this specific kind of business—as a crop reporting agency, or supplying statistics to their clientele or to the public, for examples. Here, we are concerned primarily with internal reporting. We should note, however, that critical review of reporting requirements must include external as well as internal reports. One government agency, in its first inventory of reports, discovered it was making 77 reports to other outside agencies. *Simple inquiry* of the receiving offices resulted in the elimination of 34 of these. Nobody had previously thought to ask why the reports were being made.

With internal reports, the principal problem is that they are oftentimes not managed in any systematic way. Relatively few organizations have really studied their reports and reporting requirements. Very commonly, as an organization has grown, its reports have grown with it—and usually very much like Topsy. People complain about reporting. "Nobody likes reports" they will tell you. And nobody does, if the reporting system is simply a mushroomlike growth that was never planned or managed as a whole system.

William A. Gill of what is now the Office of Management and Budget made a statement about reports that puts in capsule form a situation about reporting that managers everywhere would do well to ponder. He said:[1]

If we were to obtain a representative sample of all executives in an effort to find "Mr. Average Executive," I submit that we would prove the validity of two propositions I wish to make to you. The first I believe to be a fact. The second is an opinion or, perhaps more accurately, a theoretical conclusion.

My first proposition is that the average executive

1. Gets more data about his organization than he has time to use;
2. Gets considerable data that he does not know how to use;
3. Gets data that are dangerous to use;
4. Gets data that are useless;
5. Gets data too late to use; and
6. Fails to get much of the data he really needs.

My second proposition, admittedly theoretical but still an inescapable conclusion, is this:

An executive can be a good executive *only* if

1. He *knows* what he (and his organization) have accomplished;
2. He *knows* where he stands, in relation to where he planned to be at this point in time;
3. He *knows*, based upon present status and past experience, the direction in which he should be moving and the momentum to use; and

1. "ADP in Federal Agencies," by William A. Gill, in *Automatic Data Processing Seminar for Federal Executives*, USDA Graduate School, Washington, D. C., September 1961, pp. 17–26.

4. He *knows*, based upon past experience, that the quantitative and qualitative goals he has established for the future are logical and attainable.

In stating this conclusion, I use the word "knows" as distinct from such words as "believes, thinks, assumes, supposes, or imagines." The connotation is that the necessary facts are in hand, in valid form, and in time.

Now, you have my two propositions. Assuming both are valid, when you consider them together you find that Mr. Average Executive has to be something less than a top-notch executive; at best, he is not as effective as he could be if there were communicated to him the data he must have to evaluate the past and the present on a knowledgeable basis and thus to make informed decisions concerning the present and the future.

This, I'm sure you will agree, is not a new situation about which people are just hearing. On the contrary, line and staff people at all levels of authority in Government and in industry have for many years struggled with the problem of keeping planners, policy makers, and decision makers adequately informed. But, as I have already indicated, the people we know as leaders have not on the average been informed adequately. Thus, they and the people who follow their lead have felt the unfavorable impact.

SOME BASIC QUESTIONS

Any manager needs to ask himself some basic questions about reports and reporting in his organization unit. For example:

- What is a report? What should it contain?
- Why must we have reports?
- Who authorizes a report? How?

1. Definition of a Report

This question is a tricky one. When *copies* of documents prepared in an office are sent up the line to headquarters, you don't necessarily have a report. That is, if the original document is something the preparing office needs for its own operation, a copy can scarcely be considered a report in itself. But if a special document has to assemble a special array of information that must be sent forward at the request of a supervisory office, and if such a special document would cease to be made if the request were withdrawn, then here, indeed, is a report. This simple distinction is a good one to make, whether you agree with it or not. Some reporting systems involve only *copies* of documents that enable the receiving office thus to determine what is going on. But such systems are rare. What we're concerned about here are the reports that must be specially developed for supervisory offices and that would not have to be prepared if the supervisory office didn't want them.

There is another way of looking at reports. We can all think of an administrator who gets a monthly report on progress items of some kind, such as sales or production. He thinks of this in the singular, as *a* report. The administrator of a federal agency may get such a report. It is made up from 10 regional reports. The regions make it up from 50 state reports which are made up from 300 area reports. The 300 area offices get an average of 10 field office reports to develop their report. So, the single monthly progress report the administrator gets is made up of 10 regional, 50 state, 300 area, and 3,000 field office reports—for a total of 3,361 individual reports. Put this on an annual basis, multiply it by 12, and learn that 40,332 individual reports are involved in the 12 monthly reports for the administrator.

So, what is a report? Do we have in the example just cited one monthly progress report? Obviously not. But there is a real danger that the administrator may think so.

Some organizations have found it useful to classify reports to keep on top of the problem:

■ *Classes* of reports—internal reports used entirely within an organization, or external reports made for outside use (by the public, Internal Revenue, Department of Labor, etc.).

- *Categories* of reports—financial reports, management reports, personnel reports, and so on.
- *Types* of reports—the kind of report, as those on equipment, sales, safety, etc.
- *Individual* reports—single reports made up in one office.

2. Need for Reports

This question is pretty well answered by some of the foregoing discussion. But each report, of whatever kind, needs to be examined with this question in mind: *Why* this report? Is there really a compelling reason for it? Or is it now out of date because of change? Does it, in fact, do the job for which it was apparently designed in the first place? This presumes, of course, that the reason for starting it can still be reconstructed.

3. Authorization of Reports

In many organizations the answer to this question is, well, almost any supervisor can demand and get a report. And where this is true, the organization may be in a bad way. Note here that we are not thinking of one-time, special reports, but of recurring reports made daily, weekly, etc. One supervisor wants one type of report, another wants something else. This multiplies the number of reports required of suboffices or other installations very quickly—especially as staff officials get into the act also, demanding reports on their particular functions.

Inventories made for the first time, or after many years, sometimes show remote offices or individuals groaning under a heavy burden of dozens of reports. Any number of people in the supervisory offices may say that they get "only this one report." But the offices that have to prepare them will tell you that they must make dozens. I recall the case of one salesman who was required to make a daily report. It was put on a 3 by 5 form—*feet*, not inches. Then there was a moving van driver who had to make 11 reports on each move. Or the park official who made some 18 reports every month. Perhaps all these have been changed by now, but I doubt it.

Obviously, there must be coordination in reporting, as in any other function or operation. This has to be achieved by *authorizing only certain key officials to approve* any and every report that is to be put into continuing use. If every new report must bear the reporting officer's signature, then responsibility can be pinpointed. Otherwise it's difficult.

INVENTORY OF REPORTS

If an organization has not made a thorough and complete review of its reporting system for a number of years (say 3 or 4), or perhaps never, then an inventory is certainly in order. Besides the questions noted above, there are many others:

How many reports do we have? Where does each one originate? Where does it go? Why?

How often is each report made? Is it regular? Is it irregular, that is, only when demanded; and how often has it been demanded in the past several years?

What is done with the report by the receiving office? They may have needed it 5 years ago, but do they need it now? How did it get started?

How much does each report cost? How much money does the whole system cost?

Questions such as these are not as easy to answer as one might think. The place to find out how many reports there are is to inquire of the preparing offices, not the receiving ones. The receiving office will tell you that there's only one report—but they may get it from 10, 100, or perhaps 1,000 offices.

Furthermore, not every supervisor will disclose all the reports he requires. He may honestly think that the monthly letter he asks his subordinates to send him is not really a report. Thus, a very clear definition of exactly what you consider a report to be is necessary at the outset. A report may or may not be on a form. It may follow a general format, or it may be a narrative based on a general outline. Reports come in dozens of styles. But however they're made, they make work that costs time and money.

Timing is important to check. If a necessary report is made once a year, is this often enough to do anything about it—at the end of a year? Or should it be oftener? Daily and weekly reports had better be scrutinized with more than ordinary care. What would happen if these were made less often? Could we live with a monthly report just as well? Why not?

The effects of each report also need scrutiny. For each report, what results are there in the receiving office? If nothing in particular happens because of a report, then there would seem to be reasonable doubt as to its need. For any report, it should be possible to show the uses to which the information is put.

COSTS OF REPORTS

Once the inventory is complete, so that every report is accounted for in terms of the point of origin, copies made, frequency, location of receiving office or offices, and so on, then we undertake to determine the costs.

Determining costs of report preparation is not always easy. One office takes a couple of hours; another may take a day or two. Exhaustive stopwatch studies are usually not worth the effort. Ordinarily a sampling of offices to get an average figure is good enough for the purpose. Paper and mailing costs are usually small compared to employee time, but they should be considered. Costs of filing at both the preparing and receiving offices, including costs of floor space occupied by files, should also be checked.

Where to stop adding costs can be important. Should the cost figures stop at the point where the receiving office gets the report?

Or should time spent reviewing the report be counted also? If the report is digested, summarized, and retyped in another form, is this part of the cost? This depends, of course, on individual situations—but such questions should be answered.

Very frequently company or agency officials are shocked at the costs that appear on the inventory, not only the totals, but also the individual reports. In the example mentioned earlier of 40,332 individual reports that were used to prepare the administrator's monthly report, the costs were very high. The average amount of time spent in preparation was 2 hours per report, for a total of 80,664 hours. The average cost per hour (clerical and professional time together) amounted to about $3.50 per hour. The total cost of employee time was therefore $3.50 times 80,688 hours, or $282,324. Adding the costs of materials, handling, mailing, filing, and reviewing brought the cost of the "one" report to well over $300,000 a year. The question is, of course, was it worth it?

ELEMENTS OF A REPORTING SYSTEM

With the foregoing ideas in mind, we are now in a position to consider the general requirements of a reporting system. In doing this, we need to keep in mind that the organizational structures of companies and agencies vary a great deal, and that there can be no system that fits them all. Even so, certain elements must be kept clearly in mind if a suitable and successful system is to be developed:

1. If the reports being made in an organization have not been reviewed carefully for some time—say a period of several to many years—then an inventory of ongoing reports will have to be made to start with. This is to provide a base for the development of any system.

2. Given the data provided by a comprehensive inventory, obvious improvements can be made at once. Unnecessary reports can be eliminated, as well as items duplicated in two or more

reports. Each report should be evaluated for its need, for its periodicity, for its content, for its uses, and for its costs. This entire evaluation should be done coolly, carefully, and without undue haste. After all, reports are an important means of communication, and there is no point in throwing the baby away with the bath.

3. Once stripped down to essential reports, the system needs to be designed to prevent "wildcat" reports from starting up anytime any supervisor feels he wants a report. This is done, as has already been suggested, by authorizing appropriate officials, and *only* those officials, to approve proposed new reports or changes in older ones. These approving officials had better be reasonably close to places where reports might originate. If it takes too long to get an OK on a really needed report, this encourages "wildcat" types, and some of these will be very difficult to discover.

4. The reports official should require (a) a showing of need, (b) the content, (c) the places of preparation, (d) the receiving office or offices, (e) the uses to which the data will be put, and (f) how much the report will cost, with the proposer showing all his calculations. If a form is to be used in connection with the proposed report, this should also be presented for review. Some organizations have a form for this purpose so as to be sure that all items are covered, and the manner of calculating costs may be shown on the back of it. When the reporting official approves a report, he should be held responsible, and it should be clear that the benefits of the report exceed the costs of making it.

5. Some sort of calendar of approved reports needs to be set up *in writing*. This can show the name and number of the reports, the due dates, and the like. All offices should have a copy of the calendar. This helps to remind people of the reports they need to make as well as to discourage wildcat reports.

6. Periodically, say, once a year, the reports should be reviewed again to be sure that changes going on in the world have been taken into account.

7. At intervals of 3 to 5 years, a special inventory may need to

be made with the help of whatever auditing system the organization uses. This is a thorough re-evaluation of the system. Reports officials' work can be reviewed to see that they have done the job they should have. There may be a certain amount of duplication and overlapping—just as long as there is more than one reports officer.

8. In any organization in which authority has been decentralized, all new reports approved for use should be sent to and filed in the national office. One central location will help materially in the coordination function.

9. If a central reports file is maintained, then a specific unit of the organization should be made responsible for it, and for the annual and 5-year inventories. This will help to keep control of reporting more or less automatic.

10. The reports made in an organization should be studied by the computer technologists, especially if they are costly or in widespread use. Often enough, proper programming on a computer may make report preparation easier and compilation much more rapid and accurate. A pitfall to be avoided here is not to let the computer run the show. Some reports have become monstrosities because that's the way the computer takes them. The technologists can help here if they can be convinced that ease of preparation by harassed field men is as important as feeding the computer.

As a bit of philosophy, if reports can be made simply by forwarding copies of properly organized and coded *records*, records used by the preparing office to conduct its regular business, then reporting per se can be reduced to a minimum. In other words, if a report is only a spinoff from needed business records, then the gathering of data solely for the purpose of making a report can be eliminated. This presumes, however, that the records kept in numerous offices are all kept in the same way.

Finally, let it be noted that every employee in every office has a personal interest in reporting. What he and his fellow-workers have accomplished, the efficiency with which they have done so, compared to others doing similar work in other places, is of interest throughout the organization. Reporting is one way of showing where credit is due. Summarized reports, in other words, deserve wide distribution among employees.

And because the necessity for reports sent on up the line is often not understood by the people who prepare them, a wise organization sees to it that the values and uses of the required reports are fully explained and widely circulated in the company or agency. Where the purpose of an apparent chore is perceived, the chore can be seen as a record of accomplishment.

10

The Conference

THERE ARE MANY KINDS of conferences, but all of them involve people getting together to hear or to talk about something. In this sense, a conference is a communication device, and a very important one indeed.

Two people can hold a conference: a teacher and his student, a supervisor and one of his people, or perhaps two neighbors talking over the back fence. A conference may also be much larger than this, involving dozens, hundreds, or even thousands of people. The word has also been applied to the governing body of a church, a league of athletic teams, and various other special situations.

We will consider here primarily the conference that is limited in a very practical way by the number of people who can talk with each other. In this setting, every participant has ample opportunity to talk with every other participant as he feels the need. Several people can easily do this. Possibly as many as 20, 30, or even 50 can do this, too, but the larger the group, the less practical it becomes for discussion to take place among all the participants. As the size of the group gets larger, an increasing number of participants begin to drop out, so to speak. The dropouts are present, and presumably listening, but they may add little or nothing to the discussion. In the meantime, the discussion is actually carried on between the few people who lead by force of ideas, voice, and personality.

This leads to an important point about conferences: If you want a true working conference, don't have more people attend than can participate fully in the discussions. Or, if you do, arrange to break the conference into smaller groups so that full participation can take place.

A fully participative conference grades gradually into an assembly where one or a few people inform the rest of the group, with or without opportunity for questions or discussion. A panel discussion between several panel members in front of a large audience of observers would be a meeting of this kind. Such a meeting is not designed to settle anything or reach conclusions that are necessarily shared by the entire audience. In contrast, it is possible for issues to be settled and courses of action to be agreed upon by all the members of a true, working conference involving full participation of all the people attending.

With these ideas in mind, we direct ourselves to the three major considerations in holding a conference. These are:

- Planning for it.
- Holding it.
- Following up on results.

PLANNING A CONFERENCE

The first question to consider in planning a conference is:

1. Why Hold a Conference?

We need to remember here that a conference is primarily a communication device. Is a proposed conference the best way to bring about the desired communication? Would a written report or memorandum get the ideas across equally well? Is there really a need for discussion? If the answer is that the ideas of a number of people are needed to discuss and eventually to agree upon the solution to a question or a possible course of action—then a conference is clearly needed.

Oftentimes what may be needed is not a fully participative conference, but rather a meeting or assembly at which information is given out. At this kind of meeting, the primary reason for discussion, or questions and answers, is to clarify the information. People attending are not being asked for their opinions or judgments. All that is wanted is that they understand what they are being told. The planning for this information meeting would necessarily be different than the planning for the full participative conference.

This leads to our second question about the proposed conference:

2. What Is to Be Accomplished?

It is of major importance that this question be answered clearly and accurately. Many conferences have failed because no one was really sure just what was to be done and why. There are, of course, many reasons why people must be brought together. Some of these are:

■ To be informed. This calls for the information meeting mentioned above. Almost any number of people might come to this one; the intention is to add to their knowledge.

■ To debate an issue. Any number can attend a meeting called for this purpose, but the debate will be carried on by a relatively few leaders.

■ To discuss a question. The number of participants is set by the practical limits of full discussion. Observers don't add much; often they may detract.

■ To prepare a plan. This purpose should also have the effect of limiting the number of participants. "Too many cooks spoil the broth."

■ To agree upon a policy or course of action. Here, too, this purpose calls for smaller rather than larger numbers of participants.

There are many other purposes that a conference might serve. The point is, though, that until the conference planners are clear about what they hope to accomplish, the conference or meeting or assembly they have decided to hold may not be the best for the purpose. It is well to recall at this point that "conferences" can easily be a great waste of time if the purpose is uncertain.

3. Who Should Attend?

Obviously, for the information-type meeting, everybody who needs to be informed should be invited. For the true participative conference, the number should be much more limited. Invite the people who can contribute to the discussion, in any way we believe necessary or important. Do not invite others—observers—unless there is a good reason for doing so. Of course, we may want them to be well enough informed so that they can "spread the word" later.

If it is important that the people we want at the conference or meeting must all be there, then various problems must be solved ahead of time. If the people are heavily scheduled and travel a good deal, someone has to check schedules to find out when they can all be present. Those who cannot be present may be asked to name alternates. They should be advised, if this is correct, that they will be bound by what their alternates say. This is a small point, perhaps, but what is the use of a conference if the results agreed upon are later nullified by the people who couldn't be there?

A second point is whether the participants need to prepare themselves for the conference. This can cause trouble if it is ignored. Unprepared participants may cause a conference to flounder badly. Conference planners need to be sure the participants know that they are expected to come prepared. This can easily be done—and preferably should be done—in writing.

These two points add up to the need for notifying the expected participants about the conference. This is best done a reasonable time ahead of the conference date. What is "reasonable" of course depends on the organization involved and its kind of operation, the schedules of people involved, and the kind of conference to be held.

The next key question is:

4. What's to Be Considered?

We answer this question by making a list of the items or subjects intended for discussion. This list, or agenda, assumes considerable importance because the whole advance preparation and ultimate discussion depend upon it. It can be a hastily sketched list of possible items to consider. Or it may be compiled by asking the participants ahead of time for a listing of points *they* want to have discussed. The conference planner can use any of a number of ways to prepare the agenda. But whatever way he chooses, he had best have it crystallized and in writing well ahead of the conference. It's always well to have one item on every agenda, at the end. This item is "Other items." This is the place the chairman can put things that creep into discussions of major items and that are really out of order when they appear.

Usually, it is good practice to send the agenda to all participants ahead of time, together with a list of participants, purpose of the conference, time, place, etc.

5. How Long a Conference?

This question should follow the preparation of the agenda— not precede it. Once the agenda is made up, then approximate, reasonable time allotments can be made. This is much better than deciding on two hours or two days, only to find that the time won't permit full discussion of the topics. It is frustrating to be hurried along by a conscientious conference chairman more concerned with finishing on time than on conferring.

Also, if the conference is likely to be longer than a couple of hours, time simply must be allowed for breaks. In spite of everything, people begin to get uncomfortable sitting, they get drowsy, or they lose interest in prolonged sessions. People who are drowsy or bored will not contribute their best to the discussion. And people who are uncomfortable may become unduly argumentative and uncooperative, venting their feelings on the subject matter.

It seems generally wiser to allow more time rather than less time than necessary. A conference that ends ahead of time seems to leave people feeling better about it.

Another important question is:

6. Where Is the Conference Held?

This question may not come up at all in some situations. For example, a manager may hold a conference of his subheads in his own office or conference room as a regular matter. On the other hand, if the participants must come from a number of other localities—branch offices or plants in various states, regions, counties, cities, etc.—then obviously the location of the conference has to be decided on and arrangements made.

There are two schools of thought about the selection of a place for a conference such as this. One school holds that the conference should be held in a large city, usually at a hotel, to which transportation is easy. The other school holds that the conference should be held at some secluded place—with adequate housing and eating facilities of course—away from a city. This is to keep participants' attention on the conference by avoiding the distractions of the city. Such places often require special transportation from the nearest airport. Which type of location is picked usually depends on the tastes and feelings of the planners and participants. Both types have shortcomings as well as advantages.

7. Will There Be Outside Speakers?

If there is to be a speaker from outside the organization, the arrangements need to be made well in advance. The speaker needs to know as much as possible about the conference, the participants, any speakers appearing before or after he does, and specifically what the organization wants him to talk about. Full information on these points, made available so that the speaker has time to review them, should reach the speaker *in writing*. Usually speakers are busy people. An oral briefing is too easily forgotten. Written material can be studied as opportunity permits.

Obviously, it must be clear to any speaker exactly where and when he is to appear, how long he will be on the program, who pays his expenses and fee, and how—if this is involved—and the like. Some one person should be responsible for meeting him on arrival, seeing that he gets to his hotel, making him feel welcome.

One item, sometimes overlooked, is the proper introduction of an outside speaker (or an inside one for that matter). The best approach seems to be to ask the speaker's secretary for a resume about her boss. Secretaries are generally good about this—they take care of their boss—and usually they supply more than is needed. From this, we can select the big points. If the background and experience of the speaker are impressive, the audience is likely to give more weight to his words.

8. What Facilities Will Be Needed?

This question had better be answered with one eye on the agenda. A list of common things, not necessarily all-inclusive, follows:

Blackboard, chalk, and erasers

Paper board and crayons or magic markers
Slides, projector, screen, operator
Moving picture projector, screen, operator
Other visual aids (exhibits, specimens, pictures, charts) big
  enough to be seen by everyone
Pencils, pads, ashtrays, water
Coffee break facilities
Cards for name plates
Name tags for participants
Comfortable seats
Ventilation, air-conditioning
Phones
Tape recorder and extra tapes plus operator
Reproduction facilities (typist, typewriter, duplicating equip-
  ment)
If a report of the meeting is to be published, some one person
  should be responsible for note-taking.

The matter of facilities requires attention, even though some
highly important and successful conferences have been held
under a tree or on a bench in a park.

Some general suggestions about facilities include:

■ Many hotel blackboards turn out to be poor, wobbly, and
hard for speakers to use.

■ A paper board, with a pad of blank newspaper, is mighty
convenient for making notes that can be preserved.

■ Equipment requiring electricity will probably need a long
extension cord. There are still some hotels with direct current
instead of alternating. The point needs checking.

■ Name tags and place namecards help participants who
don't know each other to learn names.

■ Ventilation has a lot to do with success of a conference.
This point is important to emphasize with hotel managers ahead
of time—and to watch constantly during the conference.

■ Seats get mighty hard over a several day period. The harder
they are, the more frequent breaks had better be.

■ Arrangement of seats in a true participative conference is best around a round table or hollow square. Arrangements with a head table and a long conference table extending from it do not lead to participation. Further, the people at the head table tend to make speeches.

The final question is:

9. Have All Participants Been Adequately Notified?

A simple check list to answer this question would include these items (and possibly others). Each participant should have been sent:

An agenda

A list of participants, plus chairman

A sheet showing location (by hotel and address if necessary), time of starting (i.e., day and hour), time of ending (day and hour)

A notice of any preparations to be made including copies of material for all participants, if required

Hotel reservations, if required

HOLDING THE CONFERENCE

The cast of characters in a conference includes the chairman and the participants. Each has a job to do, and all are important. Sometimes the chairman has an assistant to take care of arrangements (like seeing that the ventilation is improved!) and to take his place if need be.

We consider next the function of the chairman—and we are going to assume that by the time he gets there, or the participants reach his office, as the case may be, he is *fully prepared*.

THE CHAIRMAN AND HIS JOB

The chairman of the conference is considered by the participants to be the leader. He will remain in his position as long as he leads the conference. If he fails to do this, someone else will assume his position, or the conference will wind up in confusion.

The chairman should be prepared to do the following things:

- Open the meeting. This task involves several simple things. The first is to call the meeting to order *on time*. The second is to be sure everyone knows everyone else. The third is to state clearly what the conference is to accomplish. And the fourth is to get the discussion started.

- Get every person to participate. There are, of course, a dozen ways to do this. You can go around the table in order, getting each person's opinion or ideas. You can let the few state their ideas, then call on others. You can ask one person to give an opinion, watch the discussion, ask for ideas while looking at those who have not participated so far, and finally call on any who have not responded. The point is that, if it is indeed a participative conference, the chairman has to be sure of the participation of all members.

- Keep the discussion on the subject. It seems as though in any meeting there will be one or more members who start off in various directions not related to the subject matter. The question: "Now how does this tie in?" helps bring most people back to the subject. If this doesn't do it, the chairman can interrupt with the statement that "This is interesting, but we'll set it aside for consideration later"—and perhaps make a note and ask others also to add it at the end of the agenda.

- Prevent domination. Often enough one person may tend to dominate the discussion by means of strongly stated opinions or a strong voice. It's up to the chairman to prevent overwhelming domination while still getting the opinions.

- Avoid voting on issues. This may seem strange advice in our democratic country. But where there is enough disagreement to require the taking of a vote, obviously there aren't enough facts. A skillful chairman can get a group to reach agreement in nearly every case, if he really tries, and always provided the facts available are clear.

AFTER THE CONFERENCE IS OVER

In some types of conferences, the last thing done is to have a sort of free-for-all evaluation of the conference just completed. The idea is, not to criticize the conference, but to offer suggestions aimed at making the next one better.

Following the conclusion of the conference, then, there are several points to consider:

1. Depending on the nature of the conference and the participants, some reporting to various offices or branches not represented may be necessary. Armed with their notes, plus any handouts, the participants should be able to present a full report of what went on. Better yet, their oral report can be backed up by a published conference report.

2. The official report of the conference proceedings should be put out as soon as possible. This means that some one or several persons should have been made responsible for preparing the report *as the conference went on.* By such means, the final report can be issued promptly, after any necessary editing and review in the central office that called the conference.

3. The actions that should be taken as a result of the discussions should be clear. This item would not apply, possibly, to an information conference, but it would apply to a discussion type. If the participants expect action on various matters considered, it is wise not to wait too long before advising them what actions *have* been taken, which actions *will not* be taken for whatever reasons, or that certain actions are still under consideration and later announcements will be made. If no action at all is ever taken, who will want to go to another conference?

11

Inspections

In any organization with offices located at some distance from headquarters, it is important for the managing officials to know how well the operations are going in each segment or unit. The home office of a hotel corporation located in Chicago must be fully and correctly informed about each of its many hotels. A company with branch offices in various parts of the country, or in other countries, has the same need. Similarly, a federal government agency with local offices in a number of regions or states, no less than a state agency with local offices in a number of counties, must have some means of monitoring operations in each location.

A reporting system of some kind is designed to help with this program and is universally used. But although reports provide statistics about accomplishments, costs, production, and the like, they usually say nothing about the *quality* of the operations going on. Sooner or later, one or several people from the headquarters office must visit and review or inspect the work being done in branch or local field offices. These people must judge the operations and carry back their conclusions to headquarters. This is the function we call inspection.

This is somewhat different from an audit, which in common usage is devoted primarily to financial matters. An inspection includes review and evaluation of programs and their operation, and of the various kinds of work being performed. We make this distinction here, aware that some organizations do not differentiate between audits and inspections.

To many people, the word inspection brings up visions of policing, criticism, fault-finding, and disagreeable experience generally. This is one reason why we often find inspections going on under such names as reviews, appraisals, analyses, evaluations, and other similar terms. The fact is, however, that inspections under any name can be conducted in such a way that they are welcomed rather than feared. The way they are made and the attitude of the inspector have a lot to do with this. One or two inexpertly handled inspections can often put the whole inspection function in a bad light. But isolated unhappy experiences should not cause an organization to abandon altogether an activity of great value and usefulness when it's done right.

REASONS FOR INSPECTIONS

There are two major reasons why inspections should be made:
■ They help to keep managers and other officials informed.
■ They benefit the people inspected by putting a stamp of approval on their good work and by helping them set right any of it that needs improvement.

These two reasons for making inspections should really be considered as objectives. If they are, then it is clear that an inspection that leaves the people inspected with ruffled feelings over a disagreeable experience, is not meeting the second objective. It should also be clear that if the information carried back to headquarters is not entirely correct or complete—no matter how happy the people were left—the first objective is not met.

Inspections necessarily involve consideration of the following:
- The conditions under which work is performed.
- Work going on, work that has been done, and work that is planned for the future.
- How the work is done; that is, something of the methods, techniques, and procedures used.

And finally, once these three points are clear:
- A comparison of the quality and quantity of the finished work with established standards.

These four points seem to be generally accepted in organizations that conduct regular inspections. Possibly the last point involving established standards is the most difficult to carry out. The reason is that unless the people in an office being inspected know what the standards are, they can scarcely be expected to meet them. It simply will not do for only the inspectors to know what results are expected. The people must also know, if they are to be judged against them. This calls for written criteria, setting forth what is reasonable to expect under various conditions. Such criteria should state in no uncertain terms what the standards of quality and of quantity are in the work of the organization.

Almost inevitably, reviews of actual work may reveal the need for change or improvement in the standards themselves. They may occasionally uncover the fact that there really are no standards. Conditions that originally made the standards satisfactory may have changed. The standards may have been unwisely or too hurriedly adopted. Administrative weeds may have grown up among them, in the form of substitute procedures for established methods. Inspections cannot in themselves change the standards, but they do disclose where changes are needed. They should show clearly what managers may need to do to improve the standards in use.

GENERAL PRINCIPLES OF INSPECTION

About a half dozen important principles are worth bearing in mind in the making of inspections. They are most certainly not ironclad rules, but experience has shown that neglect of any one of them is likely to lead to dissatisfaction or a breakdown in the system.

The six principles are:

1. Inspection Is Line Responsibility

The responsibility for making inspections belongs to the line official or the head of the organization. It is he who must make them or arrange for them to be made. Staff assistants participate, but only under the authority and at the direction of the responsible line official. The point here is that if any action is to be taken as a result of an inspection, the line officer has to take it. Staff officers cannot, unless directed to do so. In any case, wherever and whenever inspections are made, everyone concerned must be fully informed about the line authority back of the inspection. Staff officers assigned responsibility for making inspections, of course, are acting as line officers while they do so.

It has also been found that too extensive delegation of the inspection function can defeat its purpose. It tends to make a special and separate function of inspection. In the end, the inspectors become a people apart, relatively out of touch with the line officers who must act upon their recommendations.

It should be pointed out also that various staff officers must inspect or review certain phases of the total program for which they are responsible. This is an important part of their work, and no specific delegation is required for it. In the end, of course, their findings and recommendations need to get into the "line" to become fully effective.

2. *Inspection Compares Performance with Established Standards*

This principle has already been treated above. We may emphasize, though, that no inspection is worth much if there are no standards to start with. It cannot be useful if the comparison is between performance and the inspector's opinion of what the performance should have been. There must be clearly established standards familiar to everyone that can be used as yardsticks.

The first thing a line officer has to do is to be sure that such standards have been established. There must be clearly written policies, proper specifications, adequate technical standards, all understood throughout the organization in his charge. An advance check may reveal that standards are vague, conflicting, or lacking. The job then is to establish them, in advance of any inspection. The conditions under which a man works must, of course, determine the standards for his performance. A man selling refrigerators in Florida would be expected to sell more than a man in Iceland.

3. *Inspection Is Primarily of a Line Officer*

The idea here is simply this: Line officers are in charge of work in certain areas or offices. They may have staff help, but they are still responsible for all work under their jurisdiction. They are equally responsible for the proper performance of their staff assistants. Thus, when an inspection is made of performance in a branch or unit, the burden of responsibility goes back to the head of the branch or of the unit. Only in a supplementary way is an inspection made of an assistant or staff officer.

4. *Inspection Must Be Systematic, Regular, and Complete*

This principle seems reasonably obvious. If inspections are not regular, if people cannot count on them, if they lack continuity, then their value is reduced accordingly. If all offices are not inspected, but only some; if the inspections do not result in anything but a stirring up of personnel; if they are not part of a system of management or administration, then their value is diminished proportionately. If they are aimed at only one or two items, the emphasis they give may distort the importance of those items; if they are not complete, whatever they miss is left in the category of an unknown.

All these statements are negative. On the positive side we can say that the whole of the work must be completely examined at regular intervals as part of management, if we are to get full value from inspections. They cannot be put in second place by higher priority jobs. They must be made on reasonable schedule as an important part of regular work.

5. Inspections Must Be Recorded

It is quite obvious that placing inspection results in writing is necessary if everyone concerned is to understand fully what's to be done. While it is true that "gentlemen's agreements" are often satisfactory, there is too great an opportunity for misunderstanding, and people's memories are not always reliable.

An inspection report should contain the agreement reached between the inspector and the people being inspected, with appropriate provision for later action. This is no more than a businesslike way of conducting such work. Incidentally, if agreement cannot be reached on any item, this too should be recorded, with the pros and cons fully set forth.

6. Inspections Must Result in Action

Since inspections are examinations of performance, it is clear that what they do primarily is to reveal all the facts possible. In themselves, inspections do not result in action. A line officer has to take action on them. It is he who must commend men for good work. It is he who must arrange for help. It is he who must issue orders or directives based on inspection findings. And lastly, but very importantly, it is he who must follow up to see that the orders are carried out.

Action must result from inspection *in all cases*. And inspections need to be followed up *in all cases*. The manager who takes no action will soon find that the values attached to good inspection will deteriorate. He may well find that inspections lead only to bitterness and discouragement, and that it were better for him if he had never undertaken them in the first place.

INSPECTION IN THE ORGANIZATION

The best inspection of all would be one undertaken by the head of the agency or company. He is the one who needs to be informed; personally examining every unit in his organization—at headquarters or at any other location—should enable him to decide where and when he wants changes. Obviously, this is out of the question. The head of the organization simply does not have the time. So he must delegate the inspection function.

On this point there are two schools of thought. One school holds that the inspections should be performed by various assistants close to the head of the organization. These assistants may ordinarily be concerned with other functions, either administrative or technical. Thus, under this system, an ad hoc inspection team might be made up of a deputy or vice president, an official in charge of sales or production, and a chief engineer. They would be chosen because of their familiarity with the total program and operations of the organization. Teams like this, composed of various officials, would undertake inspections of major segments, branches, or offices of the organization.

The other school of thought proposes that the inspection function be delegated, not to an ad hoc group, but to a permanent office of inspections. The function performed by the people in this office is inspections and nothing else. They are true "inspectors."

Full-time inspectors can get very good at their job. They often spot things others might miss. Because they are paid full time for the activity, they keep inspections going, usually on a well-scheduled basis. They come to know their jobs, and they often perform very well. On the other hand, since they are not an integral part of the operating organization, they have to be kept up to date by special means. There is a tendency at least for this updating to lag somewhat; after all, the inspectors are busy inspecting. But this lag, if it takes place, is what is meant when people say that an office of inspections tends to become an ivory tower.

The ad hoc team of highly placed officials has other values. The officials learn about the work at first hand. The people being inspected are usually pleased to have a visit from officials known to be near the head of the organization. The officials, being in operating divisions or departments, are almost certain to be more familiar with objectives and operations than are inspectors not otherwise involved.

Take your choice: full-time inspectors or special inspection teams composed of fairly highly placed officials. Some managers refuse to choose; they use both.

VALUES OF INSPECTION

There are a great many values that accrue from well handled inspections. The more important ones are:

1. Morale Improvement

This statement may be greeted with raised eyebrows by people who still think of an inspector as a sort of police investigator or detective out to get his man. But a moment's reflection will show how inspections can and do improve morale when they are done in the proper way.

On the whole, people doing jobs are interested in doing good jobs, if for no other reason than the feeling of satisfaction they get out of their accomplishment. From time to time, people want assurance that the work they are doing is good. If what people are doing is not what the organization wants, then the people want help in setting it right. In this sense, every man has a right to have his work inspected. He deserves commendation for what is good. He is entitled to receive help in correcting work that is not up to standard.

With these ideas in mind, we can say that if each man knows that good work will be fairly and critically examined at definite intervals, that good work will be recognized, and that he can expect help in improving his work—then people will feel better about their jobs. Collective good feeling on the part of everyone concerned is what we mean when we say *morale*.

2. Better-Informed Administrators

A manager who is not very well informed can make decisions that may cause anguish to many people under his direction. If he is fully informed on all the work going on, he is then in the best possible position to make the best decisions, provide assistance where it is needed, plan for changes the organization needs, and in general to do a job that will make operations easier, more efficient, and more satisfying to all concerned.

3. Good Ideas Uncovered and Spread

Making inspections is one way to find new ideas, better methods, less costly procedures, or improved ways of tackling problems. As these better ideas are found, they can be spread to other offices and people in the organization. The discussions of the work provide an opportunity for introducing improved methods. In this way, systematic inspections offer an effective means for the dissemination of useful ideas.

4. Good People Uncovered

Any sound organization is aware that people are its most valuable asset. Furthermore, the organization is constantly in need of men to fill positions of greater responsibility. We know, too, that present methods of selection may need improvement— that the administrators too often must rely on opinions or impressions rather than facts.

It seems clear that inspections regularly performed can be of immense help in this area. Objective appraisals of performance can serve as guides for the selection, placement, and promotion of people to jobs more suitable to their abilities and with equal or greater responsibility.

5. Standards Improvement

Since any inspection worthy of the name is a check of performance against established standards, it is inevitable that reviews of actual work will show the need for change or improvement in the standards themselves, as already noted.

6. Employee Training

Inspections, of course, are not carried on primarily for training purposes. Yet they commonly are very useful in this respect. A skilled check of work on the ground, plus a free discussion of reasons for success or failure and of methods used elsewhere, rarely fails to increase the knowledge of both the inspector and the man whose work is being reviewed. In addition, inspections may often disclose needs for training that would help make work easier and performance more efficient.

7. *Improvement of Work of the Organization*

In summary we can say that inspections help improve both quantity and quality of work. This is the final and most important purpose. If the inspections are carried forward so that they fully justify the half-dozen items ahead of this one, and if they are followed up by prompt administrative action, then improvement of the work is almost certain to follow.

THE INSPECTORS

An inspection can succeed or fail for a wide variety of reasons. One factor of major importance is the attitude of the inspector and the way he goes about his work. Another major factor is the attitude of the people being inspected. The job of inspection needs to be carried forward as a cooperative effort.

In a very real sense, however, the inspector sets the pace. He is leading, and the values to be had from inspection rest largely in his hands. This is why we need to consider particularly his qualifications, his attitude, and his abilities. They are of fundamental importance in the doing of a job that can be useful and interesting—or a waste of time.

1. *Qualifications*

To function best, an inspector should have a very thorough understanding of the whole organization. He must be familiar with the organization's policy, general philosophy, program objectives, operating methods and procedures, and the like. And he ought to have a keen sense of the value and importance of public relations.

The inspector need not be an expert in every technical and administrative field, but he should know enough about each so that he can avoid wading in over his depth. He should know, that is, when he is competent and when he needs help. He should certainly have a good working knowledge of the kind of activity he is inspecting. In summary, a broad concept of the program, and a knowledge of his own strength, are primary requisites for successful inspection of work.

2. Attitude

Recalling that inspections are intended to improve company or agency work, we can say at once that first of all an inspector should be *constructive* and helpful in his approach to his job. He needs to create the impression that he is working with his associates to study the work, to help make it go better and to find outstanding examples of performance.

The reverse of such a general attitude—consciously or unconsciously displayed—is certain to result in trouble. Inspectors cannot afford to be "high-hat." They will encounter at least passive resistance if they seem to be treating other people as subordinates. They must avoid being critical, in the fault-finding or censorious sense of that word. They should never seem to be hunting principally for mistakes. Things of this sort are largely a matter of attitude—and the wrong attitude should be avoided like the plague.

It may take considerable effort on the part of an inspector to reassure the people whose work he is examining. Being fair, being straightforward and practical, being constructive above all, will serve to develop the kind of impression he needs to have for his work to be most successful. Every possible effort must always be made to be sure that inspection is carried on in a congenial administrative climate generated by the constructive attitudes of those who are making the inspections.

3. Abilities

Analytical ability is a key quality that a good inspector must have. He must be able to sort what is good from what is not. He must be able to distinguish between lack of knowledge and poor performance. He cannot afford to be satisfied with sloppy thinking, impractical ideas, insufficient basic facts, or faulty logic. He must, in other words, be a keen observer and a good thinker, able to evaluate facts in a logical manner, and have a practical sense of values.

Diplomatic ability is likewise essential. Inspectors need to avoid controversies. People don't argue when the facts are clear, and it is a searching out of facts that an inspection is aimed at. A tactful and pleasant, or at least businesslike, handling of discussions or questions or examinations is highly essential to uncovering the whole story. The people with whom the inspector deals are his associates, and just as human as he. It follows that the inspector needs to have developed to a high degree the ability to work with other people. It is not easy, but it is essential for an inspector to be able to draw out of the inspected his hopes, fears, and problems, and to gain the man's confidence in the inspector's interest and fairness. Incidentally, if an inspector can leave an office with a hearty invitation to return, he's on his way to success.

Thoroughness is likewise an important characteristic of a good inspector. He must get the whole story, not just parts of it, and he must know all about a given situation. The people with whom he works must feel that the inspector really goes into things completely, so that they are assured of truly constructive intent. Incidentally, a good listener gets more information than a good talker.

Fairness is an essential quality in any inspector. He must not form preconceived judgments. He must be as unbiased as humanly possible. Certainly he must look, see, analyze, and weigh, before he reaches conclusions. He will do well to realize that he, himself, will be wrong from time to time. It is only fair to exhibit a willingness to be shown.

THE MAKING OF INSPECTIONS

A man experienced in making inspections goes through a number of steps that are not always understood by the inexperienced. Certain things must be done ahead of time. Other things must be done or avoided while inspecting, and certain things must be done at the end of an inspection. The more important steps to take are listed below. These steps frequently become habitual with an experienced inspector, but they are no less important to know.

1. Preparation by the Inspector

Before anyone starts to inspect anything he needs to have clearly in mind what he intends to inspect, who is going to be involved, and some appreciation of the conditions under which work is being conducted in the office or area. The aim here is not to do the job, so to speak, in advance, but rather to soak up all readily available information so as to be prepared to understand what is found.

A brief advance review of sources will usually be profitable. Specifically, what sort of documents will he need? Will they be filed in the office where the inspection is to take place? What types of written information will be available? Will they be in the office? Will maps be needed, or plans, diaries, forms, schedules, goals, budgets, technical guides, technical specifications, manuals, handbooks, time records, expense accounts, procedural rules, policy statements, and so forth? If so, will they be available? If not, what about arrangements to get them?

Finally, a brief mental review of the six principles of inspection, together with a mental resolve to be constructive, will help an inspector get off to a good start.

2. *Preparation of the Office Being Inspected*

An inspector is an outsider to the people whose work he is inspecting. He is not part of their familiar business group, and is therefore suspect. The people being inspected frequently will read into his words implications he did not intend. He will need to allay their fears of possible dire consequences of the inspection.

The inspector can go about preparing an office for his visit by doing a thoughtful job of correspondence in advance. His letters want to accomplish at least two things: satisfy the office of his constructive intent, and enlist support in doing his job. The office personnel should be asked to suggest ways and means, dates and places, best ways to review work, hold discussions, etc. All possible of their ideas should be used; certainly they know more about their situation than he does, and it pays to win their sincere assistance.

What is done to prepare the people in an office on the inspector's arrival is exceedingly important, but equally difficult to prescribe. Books have been written on how to meet and work with people (which inspectors should review occasionally) and we can scarcely treat the subject adequately here. Some good rules of thumb, at least, for inspectors are:

- Explain fully why you're there.
- Take it easy; be friendly, and do what you can to get people to relax.
- Ask questions aimed at gaining their assistance.
- Watch, look, and listen for signs of their acceptance of you as a helper.
- Don't make speeches; don't sit too long and waste time; look especially at work they're proud of, and if it's good, praise it.
- Be considerate of their plans; *never* plan work on the week-end—go fishing instead.
- Don't follow a canned procedure. "Play it by ear," as the

musicians say, making your own approach, and seizing every opportunity to advance.

3. Items of Inspection

In the actual job of inspection, you need first to examine standards to be used. Some of these you may have with you; others will be in the office you're inspecting. A discussion of their adequacy is in order at once. You can, and should, check later to see how well the standards are used or applied. (Note that this is a different thing from the standards themselves. Use of standards involves judgment.)

The next job, obviously, is to proceed with your checklist, if you have one, of which you should have a mental image. Point by point examine critically and carefully in order to get the facts. Don't accept opinions (don't be blunt about this!), which may be wrong; get at the facts on which any opinion may be based.

As you gradually get the picture, the facts are likely to point to certain conclusions. If these conclusions are good—give voice to them yourself. It is better for the personnel to say things are wrong, after you've helped them to analyze the facts, than it is for you. Obviously if you don't succeed in getting the local folks to say what's wrong, you will have to put it in words.

Don't hesitate to depart from the checklist when you find something that should be pursued further. Thoroughness is more to be desired than slavish adherence to a pattern.

4. Preparation of a Report

The last job the inspector has is the preparation of a report setting forth the facts he found, the conclusions reached, and recommendations for action.

It might almost be stated as a principle of inspection that *the inspection report should be prepared on the spot*, not written and sent out later. This method has a proven beneficial effect on the local personnel. It goes far to convince them that the entire procedure is aboveboard and designed to be helpful. It removes entirely the fear of what the final report will have to say. It enlists the support of the local group to a much greater extent in taking action on recommendations.

The plea that time will not permit can scarcely be valid except under very unusual circumstances indeed. The fact is that time will permit, if time is set aside for the purpose. Poor planning is no excuse for not doing the job the best way known. And the best way known is to work out the report with the local staff.

It may well be that conclusions reached by an inspector will differ from those reached by local people. In this case, both can be recorded, along with the facts, so that the administrator who eventually takes one action can judge.

Finally, any inspector wants to keep in mind that he needs to work at the job of laying a groundwork of wholesome relations in preparation for the next visit he or his colleagues may make. He had better not be known as a whitewasher or a softsoaper, nor recognized as a hasty, superficial operator. He needs to build a reputation of solidarity that will engender confidence in his fairness, keenness, and helpfulness both on the part of the people he inspects and of the administrator who supervises his activities.

SOME INSPECTION SUGGESTIONS

In addition to the foregoing, experience in numerous organizations in using the principles cited and in conducting many hundreds of inspections makes it possible to list some suggestions that may be of value:

Objectives and Attitudes: It has become abundantly clear that the objective of the inspection and the attitude of the inspecting officer are by far the most important factors in a successful job of review.

In a nutshell, the employee whose work is being inspected

must become fully convinced that the inspection is aimed at two things: First, to see (and record or pass on to others) those things he has done that are outstanding, and second, to help him improve any phase of his work that may need it. If there are good things, they should be publicized. If there are mistakes, the idea is to help correct them, *not* to fix blame. If there is poor work, the intent is to help make it better.

Work or Operations Plan: In place of an agenda or checklist for use on inspections, a plan of work or operations can often be used to advantage. Such a plan, in itself, if it has been well done (which is also a matter for the inspector to consider), will provide a listing of subject matter for discussion. Generally speaking, people being inspected tend to become a little suspicious of inspection checklists. This is particularly true if the inspector does not provide a copy for everyone present.

If a checklist is used, experience has proven that it can best be a list of subjects for discussion, rather than a detailed outline; that it should be made available in many copies, and that it should be used largely as a reminder, primarily to avoid overlooking items.

Thoroughness: Inspections necessarily involve an examination of things. An inspector reviewing work should see and examine such things as training plans, technical standards, job sheets, plans of operation, minutes of staff meetings, work schedules, work-load analyses, progress maps, forms used, reports made, and the like. All these things indicate what's going on, and, of course, are subjects for discussion. None of them should be taken for granted or superficially passed over.

Report Preparation: Quite a number of significant items have been learned concerning inspection reports. Some of these are:

■ Always make the inspection report before leaving the office being inspected. Even where the intentions are the best in the world preparation of the report afterwards, away from the office being inspected, will lead too easily to misunderstandings.

■ In organizing a plan of operation for the inspection itself, always first schedule ample time for making the inspection report. Stick to that schedule. Cut out other things if necessary, but don't cut out the period set up for making the report.

■ The easiest way to prepare an inspection report is to discuss findings and agree on what should be said in the report. Then the inspector dictates it, in the presence of all concerned, the understanding being that anyone may interrupt at any time with better phraseology, a little different emphasis, etc. This makes the report, not only that of the inspector, but of the people being inspected as well.

When the dictation is finished, the job is done. There is no real need for everyone to sign it. The local secretary can type it up and distribute copies as suggested.

■ An inspection report should always contain four things in this order: (1) Very brief paragraph saying what was done, listing offices or places visited, and personnel involved. (2) A list of good things observed that are worthy of commendation. This list should always come ahead of things needing improvement. The items should be definite, tangible, and honestly worth praise. Whenever an employee receives full credit for good work first, he is much more amenable to suggestions for improving work not so good.

Next comes (3) a list (preferably numbered) of items requiring further improvement. Each item should be briefly explained. If possible, what is to be done should be stated. Each item should bear the name of the person responsible for taking necessary action.

Note that responsibility on all items will not necessarily fall on the man whose work is being inspected. Action to improve will frequently have to be taken by some other office, including that from which the inspector comes.

Then (4) a follow-up paragraph comes at the end of the report and reads something like this:

"It was agreed that by April 1, the people named above as responsible for action will provide a progress report to all others concerned, showing what has been done. At approximately monthly intervals additional progress reports will be provided until the matters are satisfactorily completed or under way."

In this paragraph, the date is one mutually agreeable—frequently about 60 to 90 days later. Progress reports go to the same places as the original report.

RESPONSIBILITY FOR FOLLOW-UP

Once an inspection is completed and the report finished, an important responsibility has been placed on the line officer. He must see to it that action is taken as soon as possible on each item in the report. Where praise is due, it should be given. Where improvements are agreed upon, a careful check must be made to see that the work is done. In a very real sense, the end of an inspection is only a beginning—of the many actions called for.

The inspecting office should maintain some sort of tickler system that will bring items to the attention of the responsible officer in an automatic way. All items should be carefully followed up until completed. If this is not done systematically and promptly, the inspection will lose its value and the next one will be put in jeopardy.

Some officials have found that if they can be present on the final day when the report is completed, this makes for better understanding of the inspection job, and for more rapid follow-up action. This depends, of course, on the time available to the executive and the importance he attaches to the particular inspection.

12

The New Knowledge

EDUCATED PEOPLE the world over are aware of the well-nigh miraculous progress in many fields of human endeavor during the past few decades. What we have discovered in this short period is said to be more than the sum of all previous knowledge. We have begun to talk about this as the "knowledge explosion." We are led to talk this way as we begin the penetration of space and come closer to harnessing the energy of the sun.

But there are many other areas in which we have also been making excellent progress. Since shortly before 1960, for example, many new discoveries were made about human behavior. This was good, solid, scientifically based knowledge obtained through the painstaking research of scientists at many institutions in the United States and in other countries. It is scarcely as dramatic as space exploration or nuclear energy, but it has brought well within our grasp highly useful answers to many critical questions about human beings.

The new knowledge has been gradually filtering into the organizations and institutions in which people work. Much of it has been carefully applied and tested in various companies, government agencies, educational institutions, and elsewhere. We not only have the knowledge, we are learning how to use it. Managers everywhere need to learn about these more recent discoveries and how to apply them to the practical world in which they work.

The rub is that the newer knowledge upsets many of our older ideas about working with people. Many of the ideas we had thought were quite sound have turned out to be only partially correct or even entirely wrong. Some of our ideas and methods have worked pretty well; it is not easy to give them up. But the newer knowledge works even better, even though learning how to use it takes a little doing.

There follows a brief review and summary of some of the major new findings, what they mean, and how they have been applied. This is no more than an introduction; a full and complete treatment would fill a number of books larger than this one. But with each idea, references are given that will enable any manager to pursue his study of any subject that he finds of special interest.

EXPECTATION

The studies of a number of psychologists, sociologists, and education specialists are now focusing on the idea that *people, more often than not, will do what is expected of them.*

As with many of the newer ideas, there is much more to this than appears at first sight. The key word in this single sentence is *expected.* What a manager or a supervisor expects from his people, he will very likely get.

To pursue this thought: if you think the people you have working for you are not very good workers, and if you expect only mediocre or poor work from them, this is what you will probably get. If, on the other hand, you believe your people are very good operators, and if you expect outstanding or excellent work from them, then you will probably get it. Whether you get good work or poor work depends on your expectations.

A large number of studies have pointed to this conclusion: that it is the expectation of the teacher or leader or manager that makes the difference. Teachers who were fooled into believing that certain of their students could and would become superior students (as measured by increases in IQ, or intelligence quotient) discovered that these students did very much better than their other students did. Foremen who thought they had been assigned some well-qualified women (but who really got women who were *not* very well qualified) expected them to produce well —and over a two-year period got high production from their units. In the same study, foremen who were told they had been assigned women workers who just barely passed the tests (but who really got the women who had scored the highest) expected to get low production—and over the two-year period, this is exactly what they got.

Both in the studies with teachers and with foremen, the only difference in the situation was in the minds of the teachers or foremen. No other changes were made. Both teachers and foremen were fooled into believing that they knew who their best students or workers were. And what they thought they knew was translated into results—high or low—based on their expectations.

Slim evidence, you might say, but there is more. In studies of executives (i.e., managers) in a number of companies, the same idea emerged again and again. The people working for sales managers, bank managers, or branch managers in various firms did well if their managers expected them to; but they did poorly if their managers thought they probably would, or expected them to. This leads to the thought expressed in one study by Yale and MIT researchers that "One of the strongest determinants of behavior is the expectations of other people."

Several questions arise here. How can a manager develop expectations? For example, suppose he really thinks his people are poor producers, not well qualified for their work, likely to turn in poor performance. In former days what we did was to get rid of the poor performers and put "better" people in their places. The new discoveries are telling us that what we should have done —indeed ought to do—is to change our expectations. Now how do we do *this*?

The studies are quite clear on this point. The expectations we have must be true, sincere beliefs. No use trying to flatter a poor performer into good performance. A manager must believe that his poor performer can turn in a good performance. He must, by his attitude, as well as by his actions and statements, convey to his poor performer that he (the manager) really, honestly does believe he can turn in a good performance. In a nutshell, in two conclusive statements from a Harvard researcher:

"A unique characteristic of superior managers is their ability to create high performance expectations that subordinates fulfill.

"Less effective managers fail to develop similar expectations, and, as a consequence, the productivity of their subordinates suffers."

How can this be? After all, isn't a poor performer a poor performer, and a good performer a good performer? The studies say not. They say it depends on what a manager expects.

If you believe in human beings, your expectations can be high. In the field of biology, we learn something more about this. Studies of the human brain have convinced the scientists that it is the "most remarkable biological mechanism in existence." Every human—regardless of race, color, sex, or culture—has this remarkable mechanism. It contains some million million cells (1 trillion, or 1×10^{12} if you prefer). It is a most extraordinary complex, of immense power and fantastic capacity. Scientists do not believe any human being has ever used his brain to its full capacity. The computations required to express just an ordinary thought are far beyond our most sophisticated computers. And don't forget this: every normal ordinary human being carries one of these magnificent biological mechanisms around with him. A little more knowledge about the almost unlimited capacity and astonishing ability of the ordinary, everyday human brain may help any manager to increase his expectations of even the "poorest" performer.

The remarkable success of Shinichi Suzuki, a Japanese violin teacher, points in this same direction. In some 30 years, this teacher has trained more than 200,000 children, aged 4 to 10, to become accomplished musicians. He never gave a test, never demanded that they have "talent." He simply assumed that any child could play the violin and play it well. After all, they could speak Japanese at the age of 4; Japanese is very difficult to learn (as indeed *any* language is), and Suzuki thought they could therefore learn other "difficult" things, such as playing the violin. Pablo Casals, one of the world's greatest cellists, considered Suzuki's pupils to be accomplished musicians. Here we have a man who believed the children could learn a difficult art, who expected every child to succeed, and who, as he was able to say, never had a failure.

The story of the experiments with teachers and the work with foremen came from the following source: *Pygmalion in the Classroom*, by Robert Rosenthal and Lenore Jacobson. Published in 1968 by Holt, Rinehart and Winston, Inc., New York, it is available in paperback. Dr. Rosenthal is a professor of social psychology at Harvard University. Dr. Jacobson is an education specialist in the San Francisco school system. This work has achieved widespread recognition.

The studies dealing with managers come from two sources. One is "Pygmalion in Management," by J. Sterling Livingston, which appeared in the July–August issue of the *Harvard Business Review*, 1969, pages 81–88. Mr. Livingston is professor of business administration at the Harvard Business School and president of Sterling Institute. The two statements about superior and less effective managers (p. 166) are quotes from his article.

The second source concerning managers is "The Socialization of Managers: Effects of Expectations on Performance," by David E. Berlew and Douglas T. Hall, published in the *Administrative*

Science Quarterly for September 1966, pages 207–23. Mr. Berlew is assistant professor of management at Massachusetts Institute of Technology. Mr. Hall is assistant professor of industrial administration at Yale. These men have also a good deal to say about the critical first year's training of new men, already referred to on pages 48–49.

The material about the human brain is to be found in *Biology and the Future of Man*, edited by Philip Handler, president of the National Academy of Sciences. The book was published in 1970 by Oxford University Press, New York. It is a remarkable attempt by some 187 scientists in the very broad biological field to take inventory of the existing state of our biological knowledge and where we seem to be going. Fascinating reading in its 936 pages. Available in paperback.

The whole story of Shinichi Suzuki's violin teaching is told in his book, *Nurtured by Love*, translated by Waltrand Suzuki and published by the Exposition Press, New York, in 1969. This little book of 121 pages contains an amazing, almost unbelievable story about teaching and teacher expectation. Suzuki's work has had a considerable impact on American universities and schools of music. An interesting article about his work appeared in *Newsweek* for March 25, 1964, and in the *Reader's Digest* for November 1973, pp. 269-275.

MOTIVATION

In 1959 a book called *The Motivation to Work*[1] suggested that motivation was not exactly what most people had been thinking it was. It had always been tacitly assumed that a motivating factor or idea worked in a straight line. Thus, if something were present that caused job satisfaction and you took it away, its absence would lead to job dissatisfaction. But Herzberg and his

1. Frederick Herzberg, Bernard Mausner, and Barbara B. Snyderman, *The Motivation to Work* (New York: John Wiley & Sons, 1959).

associates found that this was not the case. Their studies showed that there are, in fact, *two* sets of motivating factors. One set of factors leads to job satisfaction. The other set leads in the opposite direction, so to speak, to result in job dissatisfaction. And the two sets of factors are quite different.

The factors these psychologists identified as leading to job satisfaction are:

Achievement
Recognition
The work itself
Responsibility
Advancement

The factors leading to job dissatisfaction are:

Company or agency policy and administration
Technical supervision
Salary administration
Interpersonal supervision
Working conditions

The factors leading to job satisfaction Herzberg called the "satisfiers." They are the things that lead people to find full satisfaction from their jobs. These factors all relate to the fact that people want to grow and develop in their work. People want to be recognized for the work they do that they can be proud of (this is achievement). They want to work at challenging, interesting jobs (the work itself), and to advance or grow as they do so (responsibility and advancement). They want to develop themselves to their fullest capacity as unique, creative individuals. This is the concept of self-conceptualization or self-realization that many psychologists have found in other studies to have a profound effect on what people do to achieve their ultimate goal in life. When this idea is in full operation, people get pleasure and satisfaction from doing their jobs. They work harder, with greater interest and enthusiasm, and they are more productive.

The second set of factors operates in the opposite direction to produce dissatisfaction. They make the environment in which people work unsatisfactory to the workers. Unfair administrative practice (especially personnel policies), poor supervision, unsatisfactory policies with respect to salaries and wages, and poor working conditions, all lead to feelings of frustration that lead people to increasing dissatisfaction with their work. Such factors have little to do with personal feelings, but rather are expressive of the conditions under which work must be performed. Herzberg called them "dissatisfiers," but they might better be called "environmental" factors. When they are in full operation, people lose interest in their work, their enthusiasm disappears, they become less productive, and they begin looking around for other jobs (the beginnings of turnover).

There was at first a great deal of criticism of the findings of Herzberg and his associates. There still is some. A number of psychologists went to work at once to check the research that Herzberg had performed. After all, the 200 people involved in the original study was a mighty small sample of the American work force. Besides, there were only two kinds of workers in his study—accountants and engineers. There was criticism also of the manner in which the Herzberg study was conducted. All this was to be expected; any new idea, scientific or not, is at once suspect. This is especially true if the new idea upsets older, established concepts, as this one did.

By this time, some 15 years later, there have been upwards of 50 studies, involving more than 20,000 people working at more than 60 different kinds of jobs. The studies have involved women as well as men, unskilled workers as well as professionals, blacks as well as whites, Scandinavians, Hungarians, and Russians as well a Americans. Scientists, managers, foremen, executives, assembly-line workers, college students, nurses, Air Force officers, extension agents, and many others have been studied.

With few exceptions, these later studies have confirmed the work of Herzberg and his associates. They have also shown that the findings were the same for people regardless of age, sex, salaries, education, personality characteristics, race, background, and of course, the kind of work they perform.

Efforts to apply the findings in various agencies and companies have shown that they can have remarkable and valuable effects when used with skill. Supervisors have been shown how to put the satisfiers into full operation. Trained to use these factors, supervisors have come up with higher production records as well as much lower turnover rates.

It is also true that supervisors, by and large, are able to reduce the effects of the dissatisfiers only partially. For effective reduction, "top management" has to undertake this job. After all, changing administrative policies and working conditions, training supervisors for better performance, and improving wage and salary administration are not things that supervisors can handle by themselves. Top officials of the agency or company must take a hand here. What all this means, of course, is that the heads of an organization must work with properly trained line supervisors to activate both the factors leading to satisfaction and to *de*-activate those leading to dissatisfaction. Given this cooperation, the Herzberg theory has had excellent and often surprising results.

Two specific examples of size are to be found in the work of Robert N. Ford at Bell Telephone,[2] and M. Scott Myers at Texas Instruments.[3] In both concerns—under controlled conditions at Bell, and fairly well-controlled conditions at Texas Instruments—the results achieved far outweighed the entire cost of training and other operations necessary to install the theory. For example, for every dollar spent on installation, the latter company realized an average of $2.50 in increased productivity. At Bell, turnover went down, production went up, grievances declined, union difficulties were reduced, and other beneficial effects took place —in the experimental units as opposed to the control units.

2. Robert N. Ford, *Motivation Through the Work Itself* (New York: American Management Association, 1969).
3. M. Scott Myers, "Who Are Your Motivated Workers?" in *Harvard Business Review*, January–February 1964, pages 73–88.

All told, managers clearly have an important means here for improving production, decreasing turnover, and bringing about a degree of job satisfaction that may have been lacking previously. Supervisors from government agencies as well as industrial and business concerns have no difficulty understanding the theory. They will accept the idea at once.[4] Any reluctance they may show derives from uncertainty as to whether the top officials in their organization will undertake simultaneously to deactivate the dissatisfier factors.

We cannot spell out in detail here this whole concept, but managers seeking to understand and to consider using Herzberg's concepts will do well to read Herzberg's later book, *Work and the Nature of Man.*[5] This, along with the book by Ford and the paper by Myers, will provide many of the specifics needed.

PARTICIPATION

Two centuries ago in the United States we adopted the principle that our new government should be formed by and be responsive to the people being governed. We had no "scientific" studies to provide us with data about this. We were simply sick of kings and queens, and fed up with taxation without representation. We were tired of being pushed around.

Our forefathers assumed that the best government ought to be one of, by, and for the people, and, on this magnificent assumption, we produced a great and mighty nation. Even granted its faults and mistakes, democracy has turned out to be the best way in the world to govern a nation. It involves all or most of the people being governed, enlists their collective intelligence in development, and results in a high degree of affluence, education,

---

4. This statement is based on supervisory training courses conducted by the author since 1959 and involving many thousands of supervisors.

5. Frederick Herzberg, *Work and the Nature of Man* (Cleveland and New York: World Publishing Co., 1966, 203 pp.).

and well-being. In this democracy, we value our liberty and individual freedom.

Why this principle has not permeated all our institutions is a real question. That it could also produce great industrial, business, and governmental organizations escaped us for a very long time. The idea has a long way to go yet, although it is slowly, almost grudgingly, getting into our companies and agencies.

In the last 25 years, however, painstaking research has been turning up scientific facts leading to the clear conclusion that:

Participative organizations are more productive, the products are of better quality, the turnover in employees is lower, the union difficulties are less, grievances are fewer, waste and inefficiency are reduced, and morale is higher than in any other form of organization we have.

The word participation apparently means different things to many managers. Here we use it to mean that employees regularly take part in setting goals and objectives and in devising methods of achieving them. In these activities, they necessarily play a part in the making of decisions that determine the policies of the organization. These ideas have been expressed as "every employee having the chance to put in his two-bits worth."

Employee participation can be achieved in all sorts of ways. All of them depend on the attitude of the top executives. If the leaders of an organization really want a participative type of organization, they can have it. If they want an authoritative, exploitive type of organization, they can have that. But they cannot have both.

Probably the clearest and most complete delineation of the characteristics of the various possible kinds of organization is to be found in *The Human Organization* by Rensis Likert.[6] For some 25 years this psychologist and a number of his associates and students have been studying attitudes in more than 200 business and industrial firms, plus a few government agencies. Likert has

6. Rensis Likert, *The Human Organization: Its Management and Value* (New York: McGraw-Hill Book Co., 1967).

found that four relatively distinct types or systems of management can be described:

1. The *authoritative, exploitive system*, run from the "top" of the organization and with a strong hand. Employees are expected to do what they're told, under threat of penalties if they fail to measure up. The "top" officials have no particular confidence in subordinates, and there is no participation whatever. Communications are not particularly good.

2. The *benevolent, authoritative system*, run from the "top" with a strong but gentle hand. If the first system is run by a dictator, this one is run by a benevolent dictator. Employees may be asked to comment on orders given, that is, they may occasionally be consulted.

3. The *consultative system*, in which employees usually have an opportunity to discuss matters before an order is given. There is a moderate delegation of authority, and employees' ideas are sought and, when they are worthy, used.

4. The *participative*, group system, in which the "top" feels full and complete confidence in their people and involves them fully in decisions related to their work. The employees feel as fully responsible for reaching the organization's goals as the "top" officials do. Communications are free and open.

So far, not much seems novel in this simple classification of operating systems. Most managers can easily identify the systems in various companies or agencies or units with which they are familiar. The usual reaction might well be: So what? But Likert followed through with factual data proving the advantages of participative organization as noted on page 173.

His conclusion can be stated in another way: Organizations whose systems of management range toward or reach System 4 (as opposed to Systems 1 and 2) get higher productivity and earnings, lower costs and less waste, better labor relations and employee satisfaction. Conversely, if an organization shifts toward System 1, at the other end of the 1–2–3–4 spectrum, the results in the long run are the reverse—lower productivity and earnings, higher costs, more waste and red tape, deteriorating labor relations, and increased turnover.

Likert repeatedly makes the point that most organizations may delude themselves about this. He notes that an organization can and does frequently report as earnings a "savings" or cash flow resulting from liquidation of the value of the human organization. "Ruthless pressure in the form of budget cuts, personnel limitation, tightened work standards, and similar steps represent a shift in the management system toward System 1. . . . When this occurs, the productive capability of the human organization decreases. . . . The decrease in the performance capability . . . is usually greater than the increased cash flow, since the liquidation of the human organization usually yields in cash only a fraction of the assets liquidated."[7]

Likert also treats various measurements of ongoing activities in an organization. Using these measurements, he is able to predict one to three years in advance the probable trends in productivity, costs, earnings, and labor relations. Furthermore, he can discover the causes of the trends and specify any corrective steps necessary to bring about desirable changes.[8]

In addition to the monumental work of Likert and his associates, we need to mention the work of Alfred J. Marrow, who has authored a series of books dealing importantly with participation. A work that he edited, *The Failure of Success*, appeared in 1972, published in New York by Amacom, a division of the American Management Association. This large collection contains sections written by Marrow himself and many more written by 30 of his colleagues and friends.

The papers in *The Failure of Success* deserve thoughtful study by managers and supervisors. The case histories range widely over many leading industrial organizations. The whole book relates theory to practice, and is about as factual and concrete as

7. Rensis Likert, "The Relationship Between Management Behavior and Social Structure." *Proceedings of the International Management Conference at Tokyo*, 1969, pp. 136–46.
8. *Ibid.*

any manager could wish. Marrow says of participation (page 87): "It is based on the belief that workers are most productive only when they feel fully committed to their goals on the job. The degree of commitment depends on how much they have shared in both setting the goals and defining the methods of achieving them."

One of the values of Marrow's book is the series of case studies in which the changeover from the authoritative (System 1 of Likert) to the participative system is fully outlined. The problems encountered and how they were resolved, the frustrations and how they were overcome one after another, make highly interesting and illuminating reading. Discussion of failures—and there were some—is not avoided. Facts are brought together pointing clearly to the conclusion that participative management results in greater efficiency, greater job satisfaction, fewer mistakes, greater loyalty and flexibility, greater earnings, and a whole series of other benefits.

Lastly we need to note the writings of James F. Lincoln,[9] whose leadership of the Lincoln Electric Company of Cleveland is quite well known. This company used a participative system from the beginning, and it instituted a whole series of improvements over nearly 60 years. So many excellent ideas were utilized in the company that it is difficult to say with certainty just which were the underlying bases for success. However, from the beginning Lincoln used an advisory board of representative employees elected from each department. This board met twice a month, and from it came many of the ideas that enabled the company to succeed over the years.

This advisory board was a true participative arrangement. Lincoln said at one time that, although the company had all sorts of fringe benefits and a bonus system of some size,[10] in his opinion

---

9. See most especially his book *A New Approach to Industrial Economics* (New York: Devin-Adair Co., 1961; 166 pp.). The title is somewhat deceptive for a book that sets forth such a fascinating story.

10. Bonuses paid at Lincoln amounted to $19,000,000 in 1971, $16,000,-000 in both 1970 and 1969.

it was the sharing of responsibility and the full participation of the employees themselves that was the real basis for the company's success.

There are many other sources of information about the remarkable advantages of participation. The total of the studies, research, and investigations leaves little doubt that any manager would do well to consider the possibility of using this system in his own organization. The means for determining what system he now has are set forth in Likert's work.[11] Starting from where his organization is, a manager can use one or another of the approaches outlined by Marrow to reach a participative system of operation. This movement, slowly gathering momentum, is one all managers owe to themselves, as well as to their companies or agencies, to study with care.

IMPROVING WORK

There seem to be two kinds of work in the world. One kind is work we like and enjoy doing. The other kind we don't like; indeed sometimes we hate it. The work people do to earn a living can be either kind. People doing what they enjoy are often puzzled to note that a great many others seem to be working in jobs they really don't like. And those who dislike their work often find it difficult to believe that some people actually enjoy working. There is a sort of middle ground, of course, for people who like some part of their work but dislike the rest. In this situation, if the enjoyable part is overwhelming, so to speak, the worker may be one of those who "on the whole" enjoys his work. The reverse may also be true.

These likes and dislikes have a considerable effect on work being performed. Apathy and indifference can and do result commonly enough in sloppy work, that is, in low productivity and poor quality. On the other hand, interest and enthusiasm can

11. *The Human Organization,* op. cit.

result in high productivity and good quality. These effects being true—and they have been much studied by industrial psychologists—they are certainly a matter of interest for managers. If we could arrange things so that everyone could work at a job enjoyable to him, then we might expect uniformly high quantity and excellent quality of production.

Here we run up against a whole series of beliefs and assumptions held by many managers. These tell us that in the organization world it is out of the question for every worker to work at a job he enjoys. Nothing would ever get done if every person were to be allowed to pick and choose what he liked to do. Nice, perhaps, but not practical.

Many managers go much further than this. Some feel that most workers would do nothing at all if they could get paid for it. A summary of such beliefs and assumptions about people and work was outlined by Douglas McGregor[12] in 1957. McGregor pointed out that many managers have feelings such as these:

▪ Most human beings dislike work and will avoid it if they can. There is no distinction between interesting, enjoyable work and unpleasant work. The aversion applies to any work, all work.

▪ Most people have little or no ambition, dislike responsibility, and prefer to be led.

▪ Most people are self-centered and indifferent to the needs of the organization.

▪ Most people resist change and want security above all.

▪ Most people are not very bright, and they are easily misled by demagogues.

This is quite a group of generalizations about human behavior. There are, unfortunately, substantial numbers of managers who still feel more or less this way, secretly, if not openly. Obvi-

---

12. Douglas McGregor, *The Human Side of Enterprise*, (Proceedings of the Fifth Anniversary Convocation of the School of Industrial Management, Massachusetts Institute of Technology, Cambridge, 1957). Also under the same title in book form, New York: McGraw-Hill Book Co., 1960. Summarized in *The Successful Supervisor*, by William R. Van Dersal (3d ed., New York: Harper & Row, Publishers, 1974; pp. 83–85)

ously, based on beliefs like these, it is not surprising that a good deal of management has been concerned with directing, controlling, policing, punishing, and perhaps occasionally rewarding people to get the organization's work done.

McGregor went on to point out that research by behavioral scientists was pointing in a completely different direction. They were finding that these generalizations were either entirely or partially incorrect. Even then—back in 1957—the scientists were accumulating facts upon facts that enabled McGregor to offer a new alternative series of statements about people at work. At that time, these new ideas or assumptions were not yet fully validated. Today, they are. They are as follows:

1. People don't necessarily dislike work. If it is something they enjoy doing, they will perform it willingly, even with enthusiasm. If it is something they dislike, they will avoid it. This is what we have already noted in the opening paragraphs of this chapter. The idea is by no means new, but we now have scientific data aplenty that show the idea to be realistic.

2. Directing, controlling, policing, and punishing undoubtedly can result in getting people to perform work. This idea is as old as the pyramids when slaves were handled in just such ways, and when, even so, some remarkable structures were built. The catch is, though, that there are better means to get people to work. Human beings will work hard and well to achieve objectives they believe in. They will produce more in this situation than they will under the control–punishment system, and what they produce will be of better quality. Perhaps we might have had even greater pyramids under such a system.

When people work toward satisfying objectives, they find considerable satisfaction in doing so. When they can do something they can be proud of, they feel good about it. They feel that they are accomplishing something meaningful—not just in general, but meaningful to *them*.

3. Lack of ambition, avoidance of responsibility, and a desire for security are not characteristics we are born with. We develop

such feelings through experience—generally of the wrong kind. Actually, human beings will accept greater responsibility and discharge it well, under the right conditions. Given enthusiastic interest in work, ambition becomes a reality with most people. Security takes second place where the challenge of work is really felt.

4. Imagination, ingenuity, and creativity are characteristic of human beings in general. These characteristics stem from the human brain, described by the scientists as the most remarkable biological mechanism in existence. The capacity of the human brain in such respects is, as McGregor correctly noted, widely distributed in the human population. In fact, *every* human being has a brain with an infinite capacity; and no people are superior in this respect to any other people. When people in organizations get opportunities to display their inherent imagination and ingenuity, the organization benefits. The reverse is also true.

These ideas may appear to some as overly optimistic. However, both these concepts and the supporting facts on which they are based, are further elaborated in the next chapter, and in the sources cited there. Where the ideas have been skillfully applied and the results carefully evaluated, increases in productivity, quality of work, and profits have been realized far above the usual.

1. Common Approaches to Improving Work

The business of improving efficiency, cutting costs, stepping up productivity, eliminating waste and red tape, and thereby generally improving the work output of an organization, has been approached in a variety of ways. We can list some of these:

Committees or Task Forces: Set up by top management to conduct special studies, these task forces and committees are usually chaired at least by one of the top officials. Sometimes the group may consist entirely of such officials, and where this is so, a subgroup of not-so-top management people is organized to do the actual work, under the general direction of the principal task force. The people composing such task groups may, or may not, seek ideas from employees throughout the organization.

Staff Groups: Some companies and agencies have staff groups in their organizations specifically set up to conduct management studies. Some of these management staffs are successful; some are not. It depends on the attitude of the top officials of the organization toward their staff groups. Here again, such staff people may, or may not, seek ideas widely among the employees of the organization.

Suggestion System: A suggestion system is set up to get worthy ideas from any employee who will come up with one. "Incentive" payments are made for ideas that are used. The procedures vary, but generally an idea is submitted in writing by an employee, with copies going both to his supervisor and to a committee or office at headquarters. If the supervisor can't or won't accept the idea, his refusal also goes to the headquarters office where the final decision is made as to the acceptability. This arrangement ensures that a supervisor cannot capriciously block a new and perhaps valuable idea.

Payments are supposed to be an incentive to employees to submit ideas. For accepted ideas or suggestions, the employees get a percentage of the "savings" or value of the idea in the first year. In businesses and industries such payments generally run from 10 to 15 percent of the "savings." In a few companies the payments are said to amount to 50 percent, even to 100 percent in rare cases. Federal agencies are more frugal. For up to $250 worth of "savings," the suggester gets a thank-you letter but no cash. At $250 he gets 10 percent, or $25, and in the lower ranges of a few thousand dollars, he gets 10 percent. A suggester with a million-dollar idea, however, would get only $2,100.

Suggestion systems generally rely upon the occasional employee, here or there, who has an idea. Theoretically, such systems are supposed to include all employees. In practice they do not; only a small percentage of all employees become involved.

Outside Consultants: Brought in to study the situation and make recommendations for improvement, the consultants may range fairly widely through an organization, both to study on-going operations and to generate or pick up ideas of value. Some, but rarely all, employees may be involved in this operation.

This approach has one value not necessarily true of an in-house staff or committee or of a suggestion system. The top officials, having paid out cash for the consultants' studies, appear to be much more prone to accept their recommendations. Further, outsiders may often appear more "expert" than the familiar insiders.

Management Replacement: The head of a company or agency, or possibly the director of the management staff, is replaced by a new person or persons. The new man is expected to "tighten things up." This approach is possibly commonest in companies taken over by others and in government agencies headed up by new political appointees. The employees of such an organization are rarely consulted about possible improvements.

2. An Uncommon Approach

All the foregoing approaches to improving efficiency and pro-ductivity have been in common use at one time or another, in one organization or another. They have unquestionably pro-duced useful and valuable results in many instances. Some have failed either to produce immediate results or to continue pro-ducing results over a long period of time. Many examples, both of successes and failures, could be cited, and many of these are well known to managers.

These common approaches, though, have what may be a serious built-in defect. All of them have ignored, or tended to ignore, the organization itself, that is, all the people or employees who compose the company or agency involved. In a very few organizations there is an organized, concerted, and systematic effort on the part of all employees to uncover or discover new techniques, approaches, and systems better than the existing ones. This systematic attack by all the people in a company or agency may well be, in fact, superior to most other approaches. This is because it brings to bear the collective, informed intelligence of the entire organization on problems of productivity and efficiency.

The utilization of such a collective attack depends upon a series of ideas closely related to McGregor's work, already mentioned. His ideas have been reinforced by later studies as well as by their application to practical situations. Some of these ideas are:

1. An excellent administrative climate is a must. Employees must not only feel fully free to express themselves, but must be well aware that their ideas are sought and will be used if found worthy.

2. There needs to be a belief, expressed in consistent actions by managers and supervisors, in the tremendous capacity and power of the human brain.

3. The assembly-line philosophy, under which an employee does only one small part of the job, needs to be avoided. Along with this, we avoid making jobs too simple. Few people can take pride in doing a thing "so simple even a child can do it."

4. Jobs need to be structured so that they are challenging and interesting to the employees concerned, rather than dull and repetitious. Achievement must be real.

5. People should be expected and counted on to rise to responsibility. They can accept responsibility, and they will, given the opportunity in the right setting.

6. Suggestion systems that operate over the heads of the supervisors should be avoided. Instead, supervisors should be developed who will seek new ways with the help of their people.

7. Credit and recognition for new ideas should be timely and generous. No idea should be abruptly rejected; the suggester should keep on feeling that his ideas are wanted. Besides, an idea rejected today may turn out to be highly useful tomorrow.

8. Cash should be used liberally, not frugally, for new ideas. Nothing really prevents this either in government or industry except the feelings or attitudes of "top management."

9. Opportunities should be created for new ideas to be used. You don't just wait for these to happen.

10. Possibly of key importance is the awareness that it takes time to develop new ideas. Lincoln[13] had the right idea—give all the employees *time* to develop better ways of doing things, especially during otherwise slack periods. From the record the Lincoln company built from 1934 to 1964, it seems quite clear that hundreds or even thousands of human brains can do wonders.

The manager is reminded at this point that during this 30-year period at Lincoln, the cost of steel went up 300 percent; the cost of copper, 377 percent, and the cost of labor, 547 percent. The costs of these three ingredients used in manufacturing the arc-welding equipment of that company would seem to dictate an increased price for the finished product of at least 300 or 400 percent. *Instead, the cost of the product was reduced by 20 percent.* It is also significant that the turnover or quit rate at Lincoln Electric during this time was 10 times lower than the average for all heavy industry.

Hidden in Lincoln's description of the way his company generated better ways of doing things is the notion that at certain intervals (usually slack periods) *all* the employees turned to studying and devising new ways. This leads one to think that perhaps, at appropriate intervals, any organization might do worse than to declare a "management day" or an "improvement day" (or week, for that matter) during which the whole company or agency stops its regular work and devotes its entire brain power to finding new ways. What could a thousand, or ten thousand, intelligences do when brought to focus on the generation of better ideas? This kind of an endeavor would take some thoughtful planning and organizing. It would call for superlative effort by

13. James F. Lincoln, *A New Approach to Industrial Economics.* (New York: Devin-Adair Co., 1961).

the top management group. It would require an excellent organizational climate. The public relations people would love it. And it could result in newer, better ideas of real value.

Along with this concentration of intelligence, there is another condition that prevailed at Lincoln's company, and that probably must prevail anywhere: The people in the organization must want the organization to succeed as badly as the top managers do. This, of course, calls for a full understanding of the organization's objective and purpose and a belief on the part of every employee that the work he or she is doing is important.

This belief probably cannot be generated by a promotion campaign. Rather, it should result from a full and clear awareness on the part of the employees of the value of the organization's work and of their own contributions to it. Such an understanding has to be progressively developed at the time of recruitment, during the first days and weeks on the job, and during the first years of the career. What we need here is an explanation of the broader purpose, or the significance, of the work of the organization. Managers will do well to consider taking a personal hand in such explanations. Their experience and knowledge need to be brought to bear, rather than leaving this matter altogether in the hands of first-line supervisors alone.

Perhaps in this documented 30-year record we can see ways and means to develop really great progress and improvement of work, provided always that the setting is right.

3. Work in Other Countries

In the last dozen years productivity in the United States went up at the rate of about 3.3 percent per year, according to the Bureau of Labor Statistics. This appears heartening at first sight, and in general accord with the belief of many Americans that we are no doubt outproducing the rest of the world.[14]

14. Agricultural productivity has soared well beyond this, but only about 5 percent of the labor force works on farms. The figure used here is for nonfarm productivity only.

Unfortunately for us, this average rate of productivity increase does not compare very well with rates of other developed countries. The average rates for 1960 through 1973 are:

United States	3.3 percent
Canada	4.3 percent
Western Europe	5.7 percent (the nine leading industrial countries)
Japan	10.7 percent

Productivity, as used here and as generally defined, is output per worker per hour, quality considered. From the figures above it is easy to see why we are running into more and more trouble competing in world markets. The figures also suggest that the way we manage our organizations might possibly be improved by looking at management in other developed countries, especially in Japan.

An article in late 1974 entitled "Made in America (Under Japanese Management)"[15] summarizes differences between a number of Japanese and U.S. businesses. The findings warrant close attention by American managers. The article is a report by two Stanford University professors who studied some twenty-one Japanese companies operating in the United States. In many instances, these researchers say, the Japanese companies are outproducing American companies in the same industries.

They point to the fact that Japanese workers produce 15 percent more in Tokyo than do the American workers in Atlanta—using the same number of workers, the same technology, and the same procedure in making the same transistor panels, for example. They note also that when Japanese managers are in charge of American workers, as they are at Sony's plant in San Diego, the American workers do as well in San Diego as the Japanese workers do in Tokyo. This in turn suggests that the Japanese style of management may be quite usable in our country.

In a general way, the analysis of the managerial approaches

15. Richard Tanner Johnson and William G. Ouchi in *Harvard Business Review*, September–October, 1974, pp. 61–69.

points to a much greater use in Japan of the principle of participation, of greatly improved communications, virtual elimination of status in the organizational hierarchy, far less centralization of authority, and much greater concern for the employee. All these things appear to be quite obvious extensions and use of the ideas our social scientists and psychologists have been telling us about for a number of years. Compare these ideas, for example, with Likert's findings, outlined on pages 174–75.

Many managers are likely to feel that this has to do with the different cultures in America and Japan, and possibly this may be so. However, we need to note that American workers under Japanese managers do as well as Japanese workers do. We also need to remember that human beings, the world around, are first of all human beings; after that they may have different colors, different histories, different customs, and different cultures. Insofar as managerial approaches have to do with basic human behavior, many studies have shown that "when you treat people as human beings, they respond as human beings," as Stuart Chase once put it.

We are not suggesting here any revolution in American management. A great deal more study is going to be necessary before we can be really certain of how to proceed. But American managers will do well to ponder the successes of managers in other countries. We, as well as they, may profit from an interchange of ideas.

COMMUNICATIONS

To the best of my knowledge there have been no particularly dramatic breakthroughs in very recent years in the area of communications. This statement is based on a survey of the literature as well as experts in the field. But this survey has prompted the realization that the knowledge we already have is not very well used, if indeed it is used at all.

We have known for a very long time that there is a real need for clear writing, writing that is easily read and understood. Within the past 25 years a variety of relatively simple methods for measuring the readability of written materials has appeared in print.[16] The means for achieving maximum clarity have been set forth as well. And yet, millions of tons of memorandums, letters, reports, and other written materials continue to be produced with their meaning "lost in hopeless verbiage," as one expert puts it.[17] Worse, these millions of tons of well-nigh incomprehensible stuff are duly filed and continue to fill our filing systems to the bursting point.

The means for reducing this fantastic load of paperwork, and more importantly, for improving communications in organizations, are well known and are referred to here in Chapter 8. It should be emphasized, however, that a continuing system is required rather than a campaign.

In the meantime, in the area of oral communications, a number of experts have demonstrated beyond all doubt the importance of developing listening skills. Here, as with written communications, campaigns simply will not do the job. What is required is some method or procedure that continues to operate almost automatically. Training of employees must include initial training as well as later retraining in listening.

What is to be called for in the area of communications is a systematic effort on the part of managers to achieve it. The knowledge is available. Its application to the multi-variety of companies and agencies would seem to require the best of managers. Perhaps here, as in other problem situations, we need to

16. Gunning's Fog Index (Robert Gunning, *The Technique of Clear Writing*, New York: McGraw-Hill, Inc., 1952) and Flesch's Reading Ease (Rudolf Flesch, *The Art of Readable Writing*, New York: Harper & Row, 1949) are two.

17. See "Drowning in a Sea of Paper" in *Interpersonal Communication in the Modern Organization*, by Ernest G. Bormann, William S. Howell, Ralph G. Nichols, and George L. Shapiro (Englewood Cliffs, N. J.: Prentice-Hall, Inc., 1969).

enlist the participation of the people composing an organization. If managers seem unable to develop a foolproof system, perhaps the collective, focused brain power of hundreds or thousands of people can.

13

Self-Improvement
for Managers

WE COME FINALLY TO CONSIDER ways and means for managers to
improve themselves. We begin, of course, with a considerable
handicap, because managers are busy people. The curse of their
existence is lack of time, and it is time they need in which to
develop further insights into their work and to keep up with the
world in which they must live and act.

With this in mind, we need to make an important assertion,
one that is well supported by facts. This is that professional men
and women cannot afford to neglect their further education.
Either they continue their education, or they stagnate. There is
really no middle course.

The manager's continuing education can take place in many
ways—and one of the ways is the objective evaluation of his own
managerial actions or practice. He is in a position to experiment,
to test, to try—and to study thoughtfully the degree of success
he achieves. Some experiments will take place whether he plans
them or not, accidentally perhaps, or as a result of actions or
situations over which he cannot exert full control. These, too,
should be grist for his mill. The total experience he has, or that he

contrives, if evaluated coolly, can add to his professional competence. It teaches him what is wise and what unwise, and this contributes importantly to his education.

But no manager, or any other professional, can survive on his own experience alone. Other managers are having experience, *have had* experience, and most of them are perfectly willing to share their knowledge. Indeed, most are proud to share it. The sharing is done either orally or in writing. The oral sharing takes place at meetings, conferences, conventions, and workshops, where managers can meet others and talk about their profession, and where they can listen to other managers who have been invited to speak.

This sort of thing can sometimes be inspiring, and sometimes it can be dull fare. But the manager who decides to forgo conferences or meetings because some of them do not seem particularly useful to him is making a mistake. No prospector quits because he can't find gold in every pan; he keeps searching. Indeed, there is a close parallel here. There is possibly only a trace of precious metal in one stream; but there are pockets in many streams, and some are real bonanzas. The search for knowledge, of value—like the search for truth on the part of the scholar—is a neverending quest that characterizes the person of intelligence.

Besides the talk and discussion available to any manager through the multitude of associations and professional organizations, there is the written material that can be read—and if good enough, studied. Contributions to management in written form come generally in two ways. The material appears either in books or in professional magazines or journals. Much less commonly, but occasionally, it appears in motion pictures or on TV.

Anyone who really tries to keep abreast of the literature of management in all its many facets is likely to find it quite a job. Few if any managers can afford the time this takes. Even the college professor teaching management has trouble keeping up in his field, as do his colleagues in almost any other professional field.

The management field, no less than many other fields of human endeavor, is developing and expanding with great rapidity. New facts are being discovered; new ideas, new concepts are appearing.

New findings are being made by scientists in the many fields that contribute to the improvement of management. All this is happening with an acceleration beyond anything the world has seen before. This may be an indifferent matter to the manager who has elected to stagnate. It is dismaying to the manager in search of gimmicks and panaceas. It is exhilarating to the manager who is aware of its value to him.

The question then becomes: What should a manager read? How much shall he spend of his most precious time in the search for improved knowledge?

READING BOOKS

At this point we need to do a little clear thinking about objectives. What are we looking for in a book? Can we get at it without studying the book in full detail? Can we get at it without reading the whole book? The answer is, yes we can, if we approach a book in the same way we approach a newspaper.

1. Sorting Before Reading in Depth

Think about how you read the morning paper. Headlines first, perhaps, then a paragraph or two under the headlines of greatest interest to you. Then perhaps a whole article, if the first paragraphs seem promising as well as interesting. Maybe a glance at the editorial page—headings first, then a paragraph, then the whole editorial if you're interested. Then it's time to go to work. (I am well aware of course that many people turn first to the comics, the sports page, or the stock quotations. But after that, comes the news, generally read as I've indicated.)

With this approach in mind—and after all, who reads the entire newspaper?—let us look at book listings. These listings come in a number of professional management journals, in publishers' catalogues, and as bibliographies at the end of articles or books. Think of these as headlines. The few words about each one offer a further insight. If the book looks like it might be of interest, get the book itself. Get it from a library; don't try to buy them all.

Next, with the book before you, skim over the publisher's blurb on the jacket, then read the headlines, that is, the table of contents. Turn to any chapter that interests you most, then again, read the headlines, that is, the sideheads setting out the parts of each chapter. Then read the first paragraph or two, then the concluding paragraph. Skim these—meaning to look through quickly without actually reading. (Many people use the word "scan" here, but the first meaning of this is to read very carefully.) By now you may have come to two possible tentative conclusions: (1) the chapter has little or nothing for you, or (2) it looks like it's worth reading. Try another chapter, and then another, and then the preface. What you're doing here is simply *sorting* what you probably don't need to read from material that you probably should. As you go through this sorting process, make full use of pictures, charts, graphs, tables, that set forth what's in the book.

Try to keep in mind that books are written by people. Just because it's in printed form doesn't make it any better than if it were handwritten. Book reviews are simply opinions of the reviewer about the book. Advertisements are intended to sell books, not necessarily to inform you. Lists of recommended books have built into them the preferences and prejudices of the person who compiled the list—and don't forget, no one person has ever read all the books in print. Make up your own mind.

If your sorting results in a book you think you'd better read, or indeed, study, then go to it. At this point maybe you may elect to purchase. If the book is yours, you can mark it up—underlining things important to you, writing notes in the margins.

2. Additional Hints for a Reading Program

Some further hints on reading books may be helpful:

■ Look for books based on scientifically obtained information. Too little is written on this basis; we need a great deal more. There should be a basis in fact for statements made; beautiful writing, clever phrasing are not satisfactory substitutes.

■ First attention is best devoted to books that are reasonably recent, published, say, within the last 5 or 10 years. Recent books, one hopes, should contain the newest information available. This does not mean forgetting all about older ones, but there is little point in wading and sorting through a lot of books that prove to be out of date. You'll locate the classics soon enough if you do much reading; they're mentioned with respect in the new works that are themselves solid.

■ Because they want their books to sell, publishers use titles that are provocative, interest-catching, and preferably short. Subtitles often help to spell out what a book is really about, but not always. If you are uncertain what a book treats, read a little of the preface. This is a good idea anyway. The author almost always writes the preface last, even though it comes first in the book. It is frequently a rather good summary, but don't think you've read the book because you've read the preface.

■ If you come upon a book that really makes you think, and that provides you with some new (to you) information, follow up, first, by reading other things by the same author and then by getting some of the other books the author quotes from. This may expand your knowledge.

■ Any manager, indeed any professional person, will do well to accumulate at least a small, selected collection of books he finds of value. A personal library, in other words, is almost a must.

■ Pursuing a subject may often prove useful. For example, employee participation has been treated in many books. Watch for this term in book lists, and in footnotes or bibliographies in books you read. Other categories may prove worthwhile—motivation, communications, training, systems, computers, unions, incentives, retirement, and so on.

■ A book published in 1970 was almost certainly written in 1969 or even 1968. It takes about a year for a book to get published and reach the bookstores.

It pays to consider the author. Is he a university professor? Is he a retired chairman of the board? Is he a teacher? Is he simply a good writer capitalizing on recent developments? What is it about the author that may tend to give weight to what he has to say? Remember, also, even authorities are sometimes wrong. There are many things in books that are not so, as Douglas McGregor once pointed out.[1]

■ General semanticists urge people to keep three questions in mind when listening to someone speaking. These same three questions are equally valid in reading written material. They are:

What does the writer mean, that is, what is he trying to say?

How does he know, that is, what is the basis or the proof for what he has to say?

What is he leaving out?

■ Try to read rapidly when you are sorting the useful books from the nonuseful ones. If you are a slow reader, practice reading more rapidly. There are two ways to do this: taking a course or practicing on your own. In either case, you will have to continue practicing. No skill stays with you unless you keep using and improving it. Eugene Ehrlich, an authority on reading improvement, points out that claims of various speed-reading merchants are largely unfounded. You can possibly double your reading speed, but you cannot learn to read twenty, forty, or a hundred times faster than normal. "If you don't need a teacher or a machine to prod you, the best reading school in the world is your public library. There you will find all the materials you need—books and magazines. Begin with material you find inter-

---

1. Douglas McGregor in *The Scanlon Plan,* ed. by Frederick G. Lesieur (Cambridge, Mass.: MIT Press, 1958; p. 9).

esting and easy to grasp"—and try conscientiously to read faster. "If you spend as much time on your own reading program as you would spend on a commercial reading course, you can make as much or more progress in reading."[2]

▪ Following this last chapter there is a suggested reading list. It undoubtedly contains some of the best books for managers, but no one can say that it is a list of *all the best* books. It is, rather, a reasonably good starter set. The optimum way to use it is to send it to a library and ask that a copy of one book be sent you each month. Tell the librarian it is your planned reading list for the year. She'll be glad to cooperate.

ABOUT JOURNALS

There are about 75 periodical journals or magazines that deal with management. You can get the whole list by writing to the U.S. Civil Service Commission Library, Washington, D.C. 20005. But very few managers indeed need them all. Preferably, get the half-dozen or so that deal with the aspects of management most likely to be of value to you, personally.

Go over these journals in the same way you go over books or newspapers. Keep sorting material you perceive as useful, avoiding the reading of things you thing you don't really need. Skim contents and look at headlines. Read what seems good, avoid the rest. About 5 minutes will do the job of sorting. How much time you spend reading, depends on your interests.

Incidentally, you may note now and again that some new idea or technique seems to be appearing in several of the journals or in several issues of one or two of them. The idea may not seem to hold much interest for you, possibly, but check into it. It might turn out to be something you can use. But watch out for fads! There are plenty of them in any field, including the field of

2. Eugene Ehrlich, guest editorial, "Speed Reading Is the Bunk," in the *Saturday Evening Post*, June 9, 1962; pp. 10 and 16.

management. Use the three questions of the general semanticists listed on page 195, and above all look for the factual basis of any new (or old) idea.

When you've gone over an issue of a journal, circulate it to your staff, preferably without comment, but maybe with a special article here and there marked. Your staff needs to read, too. Help them.

At the end of this chapter is a short list of management journals—again, a starter set. There is quite general agreement that the *Harvard Business Review* is one journal all managers should see. *Fortune* magazine, which is not listed because it's not strictly a management journal, nevertheless often carries well-done articles on management.

WORKSHOPS, MEETINGS, AND CONFERENCES

A real participant in one of these affairs does two things—he listens and absorbs ideas from speakers, and he has something to say.

In the business of listening, it is important that a manager use the three questions of the general semanticists, which we cited above. At the conclusion of a talk, seek to understand what the speaker meant, and try to discover the basis in fact for what he said. Do this, by all means, as diplomatically as possible; otherwise you cut off communications rather than improving them. This presumes you make notes of questions that occur to you as the speaker talks. You will need to devote full attention to the speaker, as many psychologists have pointed out. What this amounts to, in a way, is that you are studying and therefore thinking about what the speaker is saying to you.

Incidentally, if you've never had a course in listening, be sure you know just what this skill is. It's different from hearing, although it depends on hearing as a basis. You can take a course in listening if you like. Or you can study a little on your own. Read,

"How to Attend a Conference," by S. I. Hayakawa, an 8-page gem available as a reprint from the International Society for General Semantics, 540 Powell St., San Francisco, Calif. 94102. Also, try *The Art of Listening* by Ralph G. Nichols and Leonard A. Stevens.

With respect to your own speaking at meetings, don't hold back because you think your ideas may not be new. New ideas are pretty rare anyhow; what other managers are interested in is your experience. Just as you're hoping to increase your knowledge, so are other managers. It's only fair to swap. Furthermore, when you undertake to prepare a paper for presentation at a forthcoming management session, you may discover that you need a few more facts to clinch your points. In getting them, you may make a second discovery, namely, that you may have come to a conclusion a little too quickly. This is worth knowing.

COURSES

As with books, courses are available on every conceivable aspect of management. The problem is to find the right one and to find the time to take it.

You don't necessarily have to go to a college, university, or other institution, although this may well be a good thing. Instead, you can invite experts on a subject to come to your company or agency. At a seminar (don't call it a training session; this turns some people off) the expert can speak and answer questions and discuss. The participants should include others in your organization who stand to benefit from the session.

Be sure to give the expert *time* to do a decent job. Some subjects simply cannot be treated in a few hours. Ask the expert for his advice on this. How much time will he need to do a good job? Let him recommend what might be best.

Seminars cost money—as do courses outside. But what's it worth to you and your associates to learn what's new from competent authorities? Some organizations keep these seminars going, year-round, once-a-month, once-a-quarter. Your people may come to expect them, and if they're well handled, to look forward to them.

Some universities and colleges will develop a course for you and your people, dealing primarily with your particular problems and scheduled to fit your requirements. They will give you a 3-day course or a week-long course, or 3 hours or so each week for 6, 8, or 10 weeks, depending on need. Fortunately, many of our universities are getting very flexible about this. Courses are going on in many cities, conducted by teachers from universities a thousand miles away.

We should note, of course, that not all knowledge is in universities, colleges, or other schools. Independent consultants and consulting firms are worth considering. There is often a gold mine of information to be had from managers in other agencies and companies, oftentimes right where you are.

A PERSONAL MANUAL OF MANAGEMENT

This is such a simple, obvious idea, it's a wonder more people don't use it. All that is needed is to get a three-ring binder and to file in it all those excerpts, quotes, and other material of value to the owner—in this case, a manager. As the stuff accumulates, segregate it by subject matter, and keep adding to it. Also, keep eliminating material that turns out not to be particularly useful.

What results eventually is a manual or handbook on management that is specifically yours. In it are reproduced quotes from material that impressed you, separates of articles, notes about books, your own ideas in your own handwriting, bits and pieces of ideas that you think may come in handy one day. Kept up, added to, cleaned out from time to time, this gets to be a highly personalized collection you can refer to as the need arises.

Many managers, supervisors, and for that matter, professional people in many fields maintain such a manual. It may outgrow the single three-ring binder and get to be a large library of binders or file boxes. Some people, in other words, save more than others. But even there, central to the whole collection is a three-ring binder containing the essence of knowledge, and perhaps referring to parts in the larger collection.

Perhaps only one thing needs emphasis—something often overlooked and regretted later. Always show the source of the materials you collect, by author, title, publication, date, and page numbers. One day when you want to write or speak about a subject and you want to quote some of your material, you'll need to know the specific source.

In summary we can say that the following ways suggest themselves to a manager concerned with increasing his skills in the field of management. He can do this:

- By objectively evaluating his own experience.
- By attending selected workshops, conferences, and conventions on management.
- By participating in meetings of professional managers.
- By taking courses of study.
- By reading and studying selected books.
- By getting and reviewing selected management journals.

Bibliography

A STARTER SET OF BOOKS FOR MANAGERS

BERLEW, DAVID E., and HALL, DOUGLAS T., "The Socialization of Managers: Effects of Expectation on Performance," in *Administrative Science Quarterly*, September 1966: 207-23.

DRUCKER, PETER F., *The Practice of Management*. New York: Harper & Row, Publishers, 1954. 404 pages.

FORD, ROBERT N., *Motivation Through the Work Itself*. New York: American Management Association, 1969. Describes the scientific application of the Herzberg theory of motivation by the Bell Telephone Co.

GELLERMAN, SAUL W., *Management by Motivation*. New York: American Management Association, 1968. 286 pages.

HERZBERG, FREDERIC, *Work and the Nature of Man*. New York: World Publishing Co., 1966. 203 pages.

————, Mausner, Bernard, and Synderman, B. B. *The Motivation to Work*. New York: John Wiley & Sons, 1959. This is the original publication of the Herzberg theory.

HUNERYAGER, S. G., and HECKMAN, I. L., *Human Relations in Management*. Cincinnati, Ohio: Southwestern Publishing Co., 1967. There are 53 readings in this second edition of this interesting book.

LEE, IRVING J., *How to Talk with People*. New York: Harper & Row, Publishers, 1952. 176 pages.

LIKERT, RENSIS, *The Human Organization*. New York: McGraw-Hill, Inc., 1967.

———— "The Relationship Between Management Behavior and Social Structure," in *Proceedings of the Tokyo Management Conference*, Session 1, Symposium C-3, 1969:136-45.

LINCOLN, JAMES F., *A New Approach to Industrial Economics*. New York: Devin-Adair Co., 1961.

LITWIN, GEORGE H., and STRINGER, ROBERT A. JR., *Motivation and the Organizational Climate*. Boston: Harvard University, Graduate School of Business Administration, 1968. 214 pages.

LIVINGSTON, J. STERLING, "Pygmalion in Management," in *Harvard Business Review*, July–August 1969.

MARROW, ALFRED J., *The Failure of Success*. New York: Amacom. 1972, 339 pages. The most recent in a series of books dealing with participation.

———— *Making Management Human*. New York: Amacom, 1957.

———— *Management by Participation*. New York: Amacom, 1967.

MASLOW, A. H., *Motivation and Personality*. New York: Harper & Row, Publishers, 1954. 404 pages.

MCGREGOR, DOUGLAS, *The Human Side of Enterprise*. New York: McGraw-Hill, Inc., 1960. 246 pages. Note also his articles in *The Scanlon Plan*, ed. by F. G. Lesieur (Cambridge, Mass: MIT Press, 1958).

ODIORNE, GEORGE S., *Management Decisions by Objectives*. Englewood Cliffs, N.J.: Prentice-Hall, Inc., 1969. 252 pages.

PENZER, W. N., "Managing Motivated Employees," in *Personnel Journal*, May 1971: 367-71.

RICHARDS, MAX D., and NIELANDER, WILLIAM A., eds., *Readings in Management*. Cincinnati, Ohio: Southwestern Publishing Co., 1972. 75 selections.

ROSENTHAL, ROBERT, and JACOBSON, LENORE, *Pygmalion in the Classroom*. New York: Holt, Rinehart and Winston, Inc., 1968.

SUZUKI, SHINICHI, *Nurtured by Love*. New York: Exposition Press, 1969. 121 pages. Exemplifies the ideas developed in *Pygmalion in the Classroom*, by Rosenthal and Jacobson.

SUGGESTED MANAGEMENT JOURNALS

Administrative Science Quarterly. Graduate School of Business and Public Administration, Cornell University, Ithaca, N. Y.

Advanced Management Journal. Journal of the Society for Advancement of Management. Quarterly. 80 pages, 6 to 12 articles, book reviews. Various special issues from time to time.

California Management Review. University of California Press for the Graduate Schools of Business Administration of U.C.B. and U.C.L.A. Quarterly. About 100 pages, 6 to 10 articles.

Harvard Business Review. Graduate School of Business Administration, Harvard University. Bimonthly. 10 to 12 articles. Much advertising. "The Magazine of Thoughtful Businessmen," and generally the magazine is aimed at business and industrial concerns. However, definitive articles on new developments in the management field usually appear in this publication. Not necessarily easy reading— as advertised by the magazine itself.

Management Review. American Management Association, Inc. "The Month's Best in Business Reading." Contains digests from various magazines and newspapers; usually 2 or 3 special features plus a dozen digests; short summaries of other timely articles; a book review section. 6 x 9 inches. Monthly. About 80 pages.

Personnel. American Management Association. Bimonthly. 8 to 10 articles, book reviews, special features. 80 pages. 6 x 9 inches.

Personnel Administration. Journal of the Society for Personnel Administration. Contains 6 to 8 articles, book reviews and several special features. Bimonthly. About 60 pages.

Personnel Journal. "The Magazine of Industrial Relations and Personnel Management." The Personnel Journal, Inc., Swarthmore, Pa. Monthly (July–August issues combined). About 60 pages. 8 to 10 articles; book reviews; help and positions wanted advertisements; special features.

Personnel Literature. Library of the U. S. Civil Service Commission, Washington, D.C. About 30 to 40 pages. Includes very brief digests of articles, books, pamphlets, unpublished dissertations, microfilms, received by the library. Monthly. Free to U.S. Government employees. Of primary (and considerable) value to students in the field attempting to keep up with the literature; not useful as providing substantive information in itself.

Public Administration Review. American Society for Public Administration. Quarterly. About 80 pages. 6 to 8 articles; book reviews; special features.

Public Personnel Review. Journal of the Public Personnel Association. Quarterly. 50 to 60 pages. 8 to 10 articles; book reviews; special departments.

Training and Development Journal (formerly *Training Directors Journal*). Official magazine of the American Society for Training and Development. Monthly. About 70 to 80 pages. 10 to 15 articles; 12 to 15 training research abstracts; classified ads; book reviews.

Index

75 76 77 78 79 10 9 8 7 6 5 4 3 2 1